Circle of Sound Voice Education

Doreen Rao, Ph.D. with Bill Perison

A Contemplative Approach to Singing
Through Meditation, Movement and Vocalization

London • New York • Berlin

www.boosey.com

Circle of Sound
Voice Education

Doreen Rao, Ph.D. with Bill Perison

© 2005 by Boosey & Hawkes, Inc.
Copyright for all countries. All rights reserved.

ISBN: 0-913932-70-1

Book design based upon original concepts and content by Doreen Rao and Bill Perison.

Design & Editing: Lost In Brooklyn Studio www.lostinbrooklyn.com
Additional Editing: Julia Fraser
Brush Circles © 2001 Kazuaki Tanahashi
Photography: © Pat LaCroix

Dedication

Circle of Sound is dedicated with love and great respect to
the art of singing as a cross-cultural, transformative and inclusive musical practice—
a *human practice* inspired by diversity, a *healing practice* rooted in ancient history,
a *mindfulness practice* for music education in the world today.

There are still too many people like Bill Perison's father, Lester,
who took one singing lesson and never sang again.

---

*When thou commandest me to sing it seems that my heart
would break with pride; and I look to thy face, and tears
come to my eyes.*

*All that is harsh and dissonant in my life melts into one sweet
harmony—and my adoration spreads wings like a glad bird on
its flight across the sea.*

*I know thou takest pleasure in my singing. I know that only as
a singer I come before thy presence.*

*I touch by the edge of the far-spreading wing of my song thy
feet which I could never aspire to reach.*

*Drunk with the joy of singing I forget myself and call thee friend
who art my lord.*

—Rabindranath Tagore, from Gitanjali

Table of Contents

	Foreword by Wayne D. Bowman, Ph.D.	vii
	Preface	ix
	Acknowledgements	xi

1 Opening the Circle: Foundations and Reflections   1
- What Is *Circle of Sound Voice Education*?
- Cross-Cultural Reflections
- The Circle Image
- The Four Foundations of *Circle of Sound Voice Education*

2 The First Foundation: Awareness   7
- From the Past, Toward the Future
- Learning to Breathe Again!
- Doreen Rao and Bill Perison in Conversation

3 The Second Foundation: Mindfulness   15
Circle of Sound Core Practice
- Core Practice Exercises
- *Circle of Sound* Vocabulary
- *Circle of Sound*: A Teacher's Guide
    - Conscious Breathing Exercises
    - Intentional Movement Exercises
    - In-formed Vocalization Exercises

4 The Third Foundation: Deep Listening   49
Circle of Sound Extended Practice
(In Rehearsal and Performance)
- Beyond Thinking
    - Singing as Listening
    - Singing as Relationship-Making
    - Singing as Peacemaking
    - Singing and Transformative Experience
- *Circle of Sound* Extended Practice
- *Circle of Sound*-in-Rehearsal
- *Circle of Sound* Practice-in-Action

(continued on next page)

(continued)

5	**The Fourth Foundation: Well-Being**	69
	Research and Case Studies	
	A Singer's Story	
	Research in Singing	
	Scientific Research	
	Psycho-Spiritual Studies	
	Research in Education	
	Circle of Sound Case Studies	
6	**Closing the Circle: Singing in the World Today**	81
	Preparing the Body to Sing	
	Stretching Exercises	
	Taijiquan Form	
	Wuji Posture for Singing	
	Introduction to *Taijiquan*: A Beginning Form	
	Studying *Taijiquan*	
	Cultivating Happiness	
	About the Authors	99
	Notes	101
	Bibliography	104

Foreword
by Wayne D. Bowman, Ph.D.

The healing power of vocal performance.

That little phrase in the preface to this remarkable book almost slips by unnoticed. After all, references to the special power of music are as old as recorded history. Music calms, civilizes, renders us more humane, and strengthens our spirit; or alternatively, it enervates, intrudes where it is unwanted, is a noisy irritant, or an unwelcome distraction. Few would dispute that music is potentially powerful. But healing power? Healing in what way? Just what is it that needs healing? Why vocal performance, after all? And what has all this to do with education?

These are tantalizing questions, and although I will not presume to answer them for Doreen Rao and Bill Perison, they point to issues that readers of this book need to consider seriously. I believe the uniqueness of musical experience and the body's distinctive role in those experiences are matters of the utmost importance for music educators. This is not just generic "sensation" or "feeling" described in another way. Musical actions and engagements are fundamentally corporeal: bodily ways of being and of being together. What this suggests, to my way of thinking, is that music matters not just because it is one "way of knowing" among many or makes daily life more enjoyable (although these are reasonable claims as far as they go) but because sound—music's raw material—engages the body more comprehensively, more directly and more deeply than do most other so-called sensory experiences. This differentiation is key to accounts of music that are distinctly musical in contrast to accounts that are generally "aesthetic" in character. Music's profound social significance, its potency in negotiating identities (both personal and collective), is inextricably intertwined with its embodied character—the way it grips and orients the body.

Some may balk at the metaphorical character of claims like these. But to evade metaphors of this sort is to fundamentally misconstrue the phenomenal and social facts of musical experience: one should not reduce music to the condition of its sounds, nor reduce its significance to mere sonorous pattern. Music is not a stimulus to which we respond, but a way of being that each of us constructs, and the body figures centrally and indispensably in that construction. Musical feeling is not something that music causes, but rather something that music, as music, *is*. The experience of music is no mere response to a musically objective stimulus: experience, embodied experience, is musically constitutive. At the core of musical experience lies, to borrow a vivid phrase from philosopher Roland Barthes, a "body in a state of music."[1] Whether one is concerned with such issues as in-tune-ness and out-of-tune-ness; with the agitation or exquisite tenderness of a passage; with swing, groove, or gesture; with musical ebb and flow, tension and release; or with the piercing or soothing features of what we call tone "quality"—one's body and one's embodied experience is paramount. Musical experience is not simply mediated by bodily experience; musical experience is corporeally constructed.

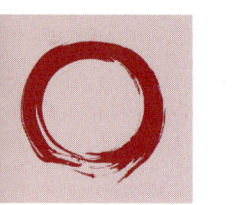

Foreword

Why should matters like these concern educators? That brings us back to the idea of "healing power," for musical experience qualifies our being in important ways. It lets us experience mind-body unity as no other experience does. It delivers us to a state of non-contingent, temporally fluid presence that we find nowhere else. I cannot make these claims for other arts, or for example, the way I experience a sunset. It is utterly unique to experience that which is musical.

Music may well be our most potent way of experiencing mind-body unity, of engaging what ethnomusicologist Charles Keil calls "participatory consciousness," in a world that conspires against such non-dualistic engagement at virtually every turn.[2] It is a powerfully therapeutic corrective to the disembodied knowledge that dominates Western societies and educational institutions, and to the confused, destructive ways we otherwise learn to think about what is real and what is not. Musical experience is proof of the fundamental continuity of perception and conception. It situates us at the very nexus of knowing, doing, and being, engaging the whole human organism, not some pathetically disembodied mind.

So *healing* in what way? Delivery from what philosopher Ludwig Wittgenstein described as the "bewitchment of intelligence by language."[3] Delivery from Western somatophobia that regards the body as a contaminant of knowledge rather than its ultimate source. Delivery from the obnoxious dualisms so destructive of our experiences of wholeness, unity, and freedom.

But why *vocal* performance? That, too, is a very large question. However, one suspects its answer would need to reserve a place of prominence for vocal resonance, the situation of voice at the threshold between inside and outside, self and other, center and periphery. And its answer would need to link these facts to the quintessential bodily act of breathing.

What does this book have to do with such concerns as these?

Simply this: *Circle of Sound Voice Education* represents an important first step toward a vocal pedagogy grounded in and emergent from the natural human condition of embodiment—one that capitalizes on embodied experiences and competencies rather than ignoring or suppressing them.

It strives to create a holistic instructional practice that avoids the destructive tendencies of teaching and learning grounded in control, fear, analytical dissection, and slavish adherence to method.

It suggests bold alternatives to traditional pedagogical practices, alternatives that treat music as a natural human fact, an essential way of being human, and a point of access to a dimension of human experience that is both unique and profoundly important to our individual and collective lives.

It treats music as a natural and universal human capacity, essential to the full experience and understanding of our shared humanity. And to this extent, it seeks to create and sustain an experiential space where concerns like value and quality retain their rightful centrality in human lives well-lived.

—Wayne D. Bowman, Ph.D.
Professor of Music
Brandon University, Manitoba, Canada
Author, Philosophical Perspectives on Music
(New York: Oxford University Press, 1998)

Preface

*A teacher cannot give you the truth.
The truth is already in you.*

—Thich Nhat Hanh

In an effort to embrace cross-cultural singing traditions and the healing power of vocal performance in mainstream music education, it may be time for us to consider alternative teaching and learning practices. New approaches that encourage deep listening, conscious breathing, body awareness, and a quality of vocalization that free the student from fear and anxiety can positively impact the health and well-being of both the individual and society as a whole. Perhaps the time has come to propose a more inclusive and multicultural approach to voice education, an approach that inspires artistry at the same time it encourages good health, cultural connection, and social concern.

Our profession, much like the world today, may be on the verge of what First Nations people of the Americas call the "rite of passage." The first phase of a rite of passage is to leave the "old ways," to separate from the ordinary ways of doing things. Getting away from the ordinary ways of doing things, we enter a new community, a new idea, a new place, with the intention to shed a skin, learn new ways, and understand what it means to be a woman, a man, a human being. As we pass the threshold of a deeper understanding, we celebrate a phase shift and we then begin the journey of incorporating what we have learned into our everyday ordinary lives.

While the "old ways" of teaching singing continue to emphasize the "science" of the singing voice, the mechanism, the physiology and the acoustics, a cross-cultural and multi-disciplinary trend has now begun. These trends will be reviewed later in the text.

Singing is never a matter of the voice alone. While the acoustics of singing include respiration, phonation, resonance, and articulation, the singing voice is at the same time a manifestation of soul (*animus*) and breath (*spirare*). Singing is body and spirit inspired by the soul and carried on the breath. Just as an ocean wave shaped by sea water represents a temporary manifestation of the sea, the wave itself is also the sea.

Like the wave in the sea, the singing voice represents a soundful manifestation of the body and soul carried on the breath and by the breath.

The 13th-century Persian poet Jalal Al-Din Rumi passionately expresses the soulful nature of singing as spirit in his poem "Where Everything is Music."

Preface

*Don't worry about saving these songs!
And if one of our instruments breaks,
It doesn't matter.*

*We have fallen into a place
Where everything is music.*

*The strumming and the flute notes
Rise into the atmosphere,
And even if the whole world's harp
Should burn up, there will still be
Hidden instruments playing.*

*So the candle flickers and goes out.
We have a piece of flint, and a spark.*

*This singing art is sea foam.
The graceful movements come from a pearl
Somewhere on the ocean floor.*

*Poems reach up like spindrift and the edge
Of driftwood along the beach, wanting!*

*They derive from a slow and powerful root
That we can't see.*

*Stop the words now.
Open the window in the center of your chest,
And let the spirits fly in and out.*

—Jalal Al-Din Rumi, "Where Everything is Music"
Translated by Coleman Barks [1]

Zen master Thich Nhat Hanh suggests that every tradition needs to renew itself from time to time in order to stay alive and grow.[2] In *Circle of Sound Voice Education*, we will explore alternative breathing, movement, and vocalization practices as a way of renewing, enriching and informing traditional vocal methods taught in studio, classroom, and rehearsal settings.

To support this effort philosophically, we turn to the ancient literature of Mother Wisdom, a powerful female deity in the Goddess tradition. Known in every culture around the world, the Goddess tradition offers us access to original thinking without the limitations of gender differentiation or sharp individuation of any kind. Mother Wisdom stood outside frameworks, yet her unifying wisdom presented ways of harmonizing traditions and practices that advanced rival claims. By her nature she was always global.

In the spirit of the Goddess tradition, the new century of voice education likely starts with a cross-cultural, multi-disciplinary view of singing—a view that goes beyond the limitations of oppositional, dualistic thinking and embraces the diversity of teaching practices that enrich the quality of musical experience for all developing singers; a view of voice education that harmonizes the Eastern contemplative practices of breathing meditation and martial arts movement with Western European bel canto techniques; a view that links the art of singing with the health of the mind and body; a view supported by the most advanced scientific research today; a view that takes into consideration the socially and spiritually relevant realities and opportunities available in the 21st century.

We acknowledge that our exploratory efforts to link diverse traditions and practices in the realm of voice education may ruffle a few feathers and raise some eyebrows among our classically oriented colleagues. We hope however that our readers will understand that we are on a journey to find new ways of expanding the practice of voice education inclusive of ancient and cross-cultural traditions, psycho-spiritual considerations, and scientific research.

We once heard the Dalai Lama say "there are five billion people in the world, so there are five billion points of view." So, we don't expect our readers to necessarily embrace the entire contents of this book without careful consideration. We do ask you, however, to remember the last three lines of Rumi's wonderful poem "Where Everything is Music":

*Stop the words now.
Open the window in the center of your chest,
And let the spirits fly in and out.*

Acknowledgements

Linking contemplative traditions and unifying diverse educational practices in an effort to renew and deepen our understanding of voice education is a daunting task. This particular effort could only be undertaken by two radical optimists who learned in the process of trying to complete this book, to cooperate with the inevitable. Because the *Circle of Sound Voice Education* practice and this inaugural publication project evolved over a period of six years, Bill and I have many people to thank.

As the primary author of this text, it is a privilege for me to begin these acknowledgements by thanking Professor David Elliott, author of *Music Matters: A New Philosophy of Music Education* and David's mentor, Emeritus Professor Bennett Reimer, author of *A Philosophy of Music Education*. Both these colleagues provided the music education profession with important philosophical perspectives, David on the nature and value of performance in music education, Bennett on the nature and value of aesthetic education as music education. However, neither author fully acknowledges the worldwide trend of the present generation of students to be more troubled emotionally, more lonely, depressed and worried than past generations. Neither author addresses music in education as an effort to inculcate essential human values such as self-awareness, the art of deep listening and the role of musical experience for health and well-being.

For this reason I made the decision to cross disciplines and explore indigenous circle cultures, meditation practices, and the martial arts in relation to music performance in education, work that continues my doctoral research on the emotional and psycho-spiritual nature of singing. Over a six-year period of research and writing, I went to the desert of the Southwestern United States, the Ganges River in India, and the Himalayan Mountains of Bhutan to observe the "big picture" and to study the way the singing voice is used cross-culturally around the world. While these teachings were not always easy, I feel a deep gratitude to both David Elliott and Bennett Reimer for giving impetus to my journey to understand the nature and value of musical experience *beyond thinking*.

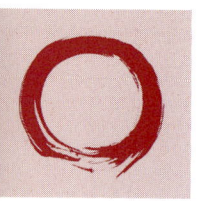

Acknowledgements

Bill Perison and I want to acknowledge the children of the North York Region of the Toronto District School Board and former North York Music Coordinator Elaine Mason. In an effort to revitalize choral singing in the public schools, Bill and I worked with the students of North York, field testing each stage of the *Circle of Sound Voice Education* method. We are also grateful to the hundreds of choral teachers in the United States, Canada, and Europe who embraced this emerging practice and thoughtfully integrated *Circle of Sound Voice Education* into their studios, classrooms, and choral rehearsals. Samplings of their stories are detailed in Chapter 5.

Circle of Sound has traveled the world, enthusiastically received in many different countries including the Philippines, Singapore, Norway, Sweden, Australia, England, Scotland, Ireland and many other places. We are grateful to all those professional singers and teachers who "suspended their disbelief" and willingly experimented, explored and affirmed the effectiveness of this contemplative approach to singing.

My colleagues at the University of Toronto, particularly Professor Lori Dolloff, Dean David Beach, and Professor Lorna MacDonald, the Lois Marshall Chair of Voice Studies, were more than encouraging to me during this extended period of research and writing. Bill and I are especially grateful to our CME Associate Lori Dolloff for her personal interest in this work and for the time she contributed to developing the "In Conversation" segment found in Chapter 2. I am indebted to the University of Toronto MacMillan Singers, my perceptive and talented choir who showed me time and time again how important it was to start choir rehearsals with mindfulness meditation.

Bill's family—Dianne, Austin and Liam—endured long periods of Bill's absence as he traveled across Canada and Europe to collaborate with me during the field testing and writing of this book. As the *Circle of Sound* practice emerged and as this writing came to completion, so did my son Rajeev's good health. It seems that the contemplative arts, the healing arts and the vocal arts share much in common.

In deepest gratitude I thank my meditation teachers, the Venerable Thay Thich Nhat Hahn in Plum Village France and Joan Halifax Roshi at Upaya Zen Center in Santa Fe, New Mexico. I also bow in deep gratitude to Kazuaki Tanahashi Sensei of the San Francisco Zen Center, not only for his Brush Circles seen throughout this book, and his Buddhist scholarship enjoyed throughout the world, but for his abiding friendship and faith in my work.

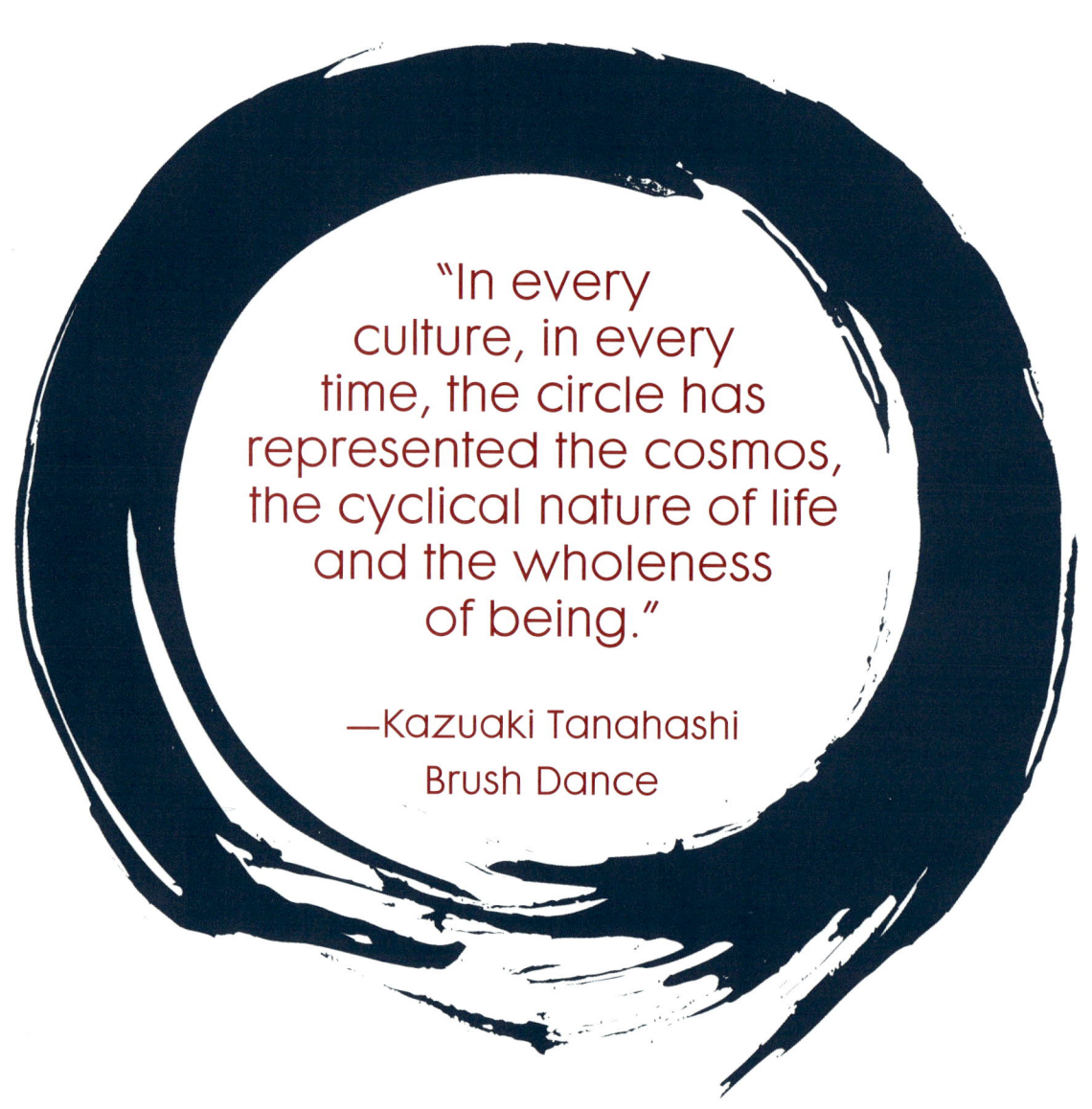

"In every culture, in every time, the circle has represented the cosmos, the cyclical nature of life and the wholeness of being."

—Kazuaki Tanahashi
Brush Dance

Chapter 1
Opening the Circle: Foundations and Reflections

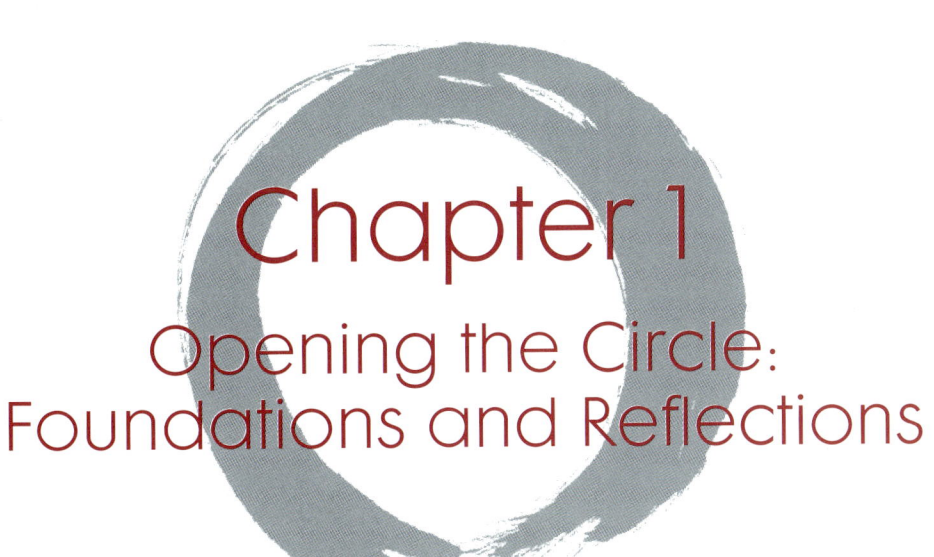

What is Circle of Sound Voice Education?

Circle of Sound is a contemplative or "mindfulness" approach to voice education. This versatile approach to singing blends conscious breathing exercises, derived from Eastern meditation techniques, and martial arts movement practices adapted from *taijiquan* (t'ai chi ch'uan) with Western bel canto vocalization. The breathing, movement, and vocalization exercises have been carefully adapted from their original forms for use in a variety of teaching and learning environments. Wherever there is a sincere interest in helping students access their singing voices in a conscious, intentional, and in-formed manner, *Circle of Sound* will work successfully.

Easily integrated into traditional studio, classroom and rehearsal settings as an easy series of warm-up exercises, the *Circle of Sound* approach to voice education emerged in an effort to find new ways of freeing the singer from the fears and anxieties often associated with the desire to produce the "perfect" or "ideal" tone quality. A versatile and healthful way of enriching traditional voice methods, *Circle of Sound* also supports the development of calm, ease and concentration during singing.

By describing *Circle of Sound* as a "contemplative approach" to singing, we are suggesting a certain quality of thoughtfulness or mindfulness that is often associated with meditation or conscious breathing. The breathing exercises are designed to inspire a dynamic quality of "deep listening" that allows the singers to hear themselves and others. Used systematically, on a regular basis, the singer's concentration and awareness deepens dramatically in a relatively short period of time. Eventually, the singer's focus drops from the head into the heart "where everything is music." (Rumi)

Circle of Sound is an inclusive teaching and learning practice for the voice education of children and adults, beginners through advanced singers. Based on Doreen Rao's *Choral Music Experience* performance approach to music education,[1] *Circle of Sound* views singing as a multidimensional practice of deep listening, bodily awareness, mindfulness, and self understanding. Developed over many years of research, performing, and teaching, *Circle of Sound Voice Education* has been described by professionals and students alike as a holistic, organic, and healthful approach to singing.

In *Circle of Sound*, developing singers are viewed as their own best teachers. Students learn meaningfully from the sounds and feelings of their own lives, experiences, successes, and failures. Learning to sing from the "inside out," students begin to replace the fear and anxiety that comes from trying to "control" or "coordinate" vocal tone, or from trying to sound like other "more acceptable" singing voices, with a sense of self-trust, well-being, and equanimity or "letting go." Through the systematic practice of "mindfulness"—

Opening the Circle

a deep awareness that comes from conscious breathing—singers learn to trust the quality of their own experiences. The singing voice develops naturally as a form of deep listening and personal insight.

Through a systematic, integrated, and detailed series of exercises shown throughout the text, the authors hope to serve as your coaches and *Circle of Sound Voice Education* guides. Together, we will practice conscious breathing, intentional movement, and in-formed vocalization—the "core practice" of awakening your true voice and recognizing that you already are the singer you want to become. The true meaning of *Circle of Sound* cannot be adequately described in words. It must be practiced.

Cross-Cultural Reflections

In 1986, Finnish conductor and music educator Erkki Pohjola invited me to bring the Glen Ellyn Children's Chorus from Chicago to Helsinki as guests of his Tapiola Choir. With nine other young choirs from around the world, the Glen Ellyn Children's Chorus was honored to participate in the First International Choral Symppatti in Helsinki's Finlandia Hall. Between rehearsals, concerts, and television broadcasts, Finlandia Hall's backstage was bustling with young singers and conductors enthusiastically exchanging songs, stories, dances, and dreams of the future.

During those precious backstage moments, I was aware of the quiet, purposeful, dance-like movements being made in one corner by a Japanese conductor. Quiet filled me as I watched the slow, concentrated shaping of his carefully crafted, coordinated movements. Back on the concert stage, his conducting leadership was dynamic, precise, and compelling. The symphonic-size Japanese choir sang as one voice, demonstrating an astounding and contrasting range of expressive capabilities. Their Helsinki performance stuck to my musical bones for years afterwards. I can still recall the lyrical melodies, the exacting rhythms, and the luscious sonorities of each piece performed by the young Japanese singers.

The Helsinki Choral Symppatti, and many other cross-cultural performances and teaching experiences since, have caused me to examine my own beliefs about the nature and value of voice education. The unity, quiet, and deep concentration of the Japanese choir, the strong sense of social and cultural identity of the Scandinavian and Baltic choirs, and the passionate life-or-death performance style of the Israeli choir inspired my continued quest for understanding the value of singing from a cross-cultural perspective.

In eastern Europe, Finland, and the Baltics, for example, there appears to be a strong sense of personal, cultural, and social identity in choral singing. The repertoire performed in these regions reflects a creative use of historic and political themes, as well as a deep respect for the contemporary music of living composers, whom they honor at every opportunity. The singers appear confident and at ease with their musical identities, as related to and inseparable from their nation's political and social agendas. The quality of the "Baltic vocalism" is stunningly resonant, inherently passionate, and strong.

In many African cultures, including the Ewe of Ghana, the Shona of Zimbabwe, and the Zulu of South Africa, singing as a way of life forms the basis for family and community ritual and ceremony. There is little separation between singing and everyday life. Concert halls do not divide or separate those who sing, drum, and dance from the rest of the community. The warm, "pushed," and deeply resonant singing of many black Africans is used without the baggage of aesthetic orientation or self-doubt so often inherent in Western European singing traditions.

Amongst indigenous cultures I have known, including the Sami of Scandinavia, the Aborigines of Australia, and First Nations of the Americas, singing is used therapeutically as a form of medicine and healing to remedy emotional and physical illness. Holy men and women, sound healers, and indigenous healers throughout the world practice singing to affect human consciousness and improve health. For indigenous healers or shamans, the concept of tonal aesthetic does not exist. Sustaining life is what counts.

Opening the Circle

This vision song was sung to a woman when she was sick. She then used it to heal others.

> *In your throat is a living song*
> *A living spirit song*
> *Her name is Long-Life-Maker*
>
> *Yes I'm here to heal*
> *With the healing ways*
> *Of the Magic-of-the-Ground*
> *The Magic-of-the-Earth*
>
> *So go on poor friend*
> *And sing with the healing spirit*
> *With the Magic-of-the-Ground*
> *The Magic-of-the-Earth*
>
> *And you will spring to life*
> *Through the power of the words*
> *Through the Magic-of-the Ground*
> *The Magic-of-the-Earth*[2]

These cross-cultural descriptions of singing from a variety of different traditions provide a rich palette of contrasting perspectives. From these examples and many others in the world today, we can examine the role of singing and vocal performance in music education and in everyday life. What is the value of learning to sing in the world of today? Is the value of singing aesthetic experience, social identity, physical health, psychological well-being, or spiritual enlightenment? Is singing a demonstration of artistry or musicianship, is it the formation of consciousness, or is it a manifestation of the soul?

As performers, teachers, and health care professionals continue to investigate the power of singing in relation to the wholeness of body, mind, and spirit, these questions can serve as a guide to the future of alternative theories and practices associated with singing and voice education. As psychiatrist Carl Jung said to concert pianist and music therapist Margaret Tilly in response to her pioneering work using musical performance therapeutically, "this opens up whole new avenues of research I'd never even dreamed of."[3]

The Circle Image

In a committed effort to rethink the nature and value of vocal music education in relation to its diverse social contexts and its psycho-spiritual dimensions, I began to investigate the contemplative arts. Through my own contemplative efforts, I started exploring potential intersections between Eastern meditation and martial arts practices and Western European singing traditions.

During an extended period of research, I developed an interest in circles as mystic images and sacred symbols. Dating back to the Paleolithic period and represented by some indigenous cultures as the Medicine Wheel, the circle was carved and painted as a sacred symbol thousands of years before the wheel was invented as a tool. In ancient times, circle-based social structures thrived in many communities around the world. Circle-based culture still exists among some indigenous peoples in isolated locations, including the Inuit of the Canadian Arctic, the Aborigines of Australia, the Zulu of South Africa, and the Plains people of the United States.

The image of circle and circularity is closely connected to the kind of dynamic and interactive teaching style I have always appreciated. However, circle is not just a way of setting up chairs for voice class or choir practice. The circle phenomenon is a way of imagining every aspect of voice teaching and learning. While the circle image may seem new or unusual to most of us, this form of imagining incorporates the ways of many diverse cultures, ancient and modern.

In a musical context, the circle image is related to the dynamic qualities of sound vibrations and vocal acoustics. The open spaces of the singer's vocal tract, for example, can be imaged as a "circle space" created vertically by the raised soft palate and the lowered larynx, and horizontally by the widened pharynx. The acoustical environment of the vocal tract,

Opening the Circle

or voice resonance chamber, can be imagined as a circle or circle space.

Educationally, the circle image is about equalizing the quality of teaching and learning relationships. It is about caring for others. In a teaching and learning circle, like the indigenous way of council, all are beautiful, all are equal in beauty, all are heard as beautiful. The "learning circle" is a sacred space for listening to what the singing voice is telling us. The circle encourages members of the teaching and learning community to bear witness to whatever the singing voice wants to sound like in that moment. Circle is "where mind widens out and merges into the mind of mankind—where we are all one."[4]

The educational application of the circle image for voice education became clear to me during a week-long wilderness fast when I was camping alone in the Santa Fe National Forest in New Mexico. Singing became an important part of my physical and emotional survival. In the desert, an image emerged of the singing voice as the "circle within"—a microcosm of the universe expanding and connecting through musical experience. Certainly the acoustics and physiology of the voice tract as a lowered larynx, lifted soft palate, and widened pharynx, as we know it scientifically, could also be thought of metaphysically as an infinite and sustainable source of space—a circle space for listening, a circle space for singing, and a circle space for understanding.

As I learned to listen to the singing voice as the circle within, I came to a place Zen students call "not-knowing." Not-knowing is a way of listening deeply without judgment. It could also be described as "beginner's mind" or as a way of looking through innocent-eyes. Philosophy has many terms to describe this method of inquiry including what is known as phenomenological method. Experimental research relies on not-knowing as a form of exercising objectivity. I prefer to use an experientially derived vocabulary that connects more intimately with the lived experience.

Practicing "not-knowing" allows the singer to receive ideas and information in a more inclusive and non-judgmental spirit. While it may seem unusual for someone to write a book from this kind of perspective, it is my beginner's mind that encourages me to share this contemplative approach to singing with my friends and colleagues. With a "beginner's mind," it is easier for us to observe ourselves, our singing, our fellow singers and those for whom we sing.

In summary, not all aspects of singing are as metaphysical as this particular narrative on circle image might suggest. Years of field-testing *Circle of Sound Voice Education* revealed a complete synergy between this contemplative approach to singing and the science of vocal acoustics and physiology. The instructional and psychological benefits of this field-testing produced a revealing response from singers, teachers, and conductors worldwide (see case studies in Chapter 5).

Finally, please let me remind you about the inherent limitations of learning the *Circle of Sound Voice Education* approach from this text alone. It is important to remember that the written information does not constitute the practice. We encourage you to begin practicing slowly and thoughtfully, in little bits, as needed, and as it works for you.

In the words of philosopher and esteemed Canadian colleague Francis Sparshott, "A system of apprehended truths is not the same as the ability to turn out a product."[5] Professor Sparshott also reminds us that "the joy of doing, of being aware of what one is doing, is a primary kind of aesthetic delight whose importance no theorist of art must forget."[6]

Opening the Circle

The Four Foundations of Circle of Sound Voice Education

Circle of Sound Voice Education is based on four important elements that serve as the foundation for this teaching philosophy and singing practice. The same four foundations also form the basis of this instructional guide.

The First Foundation: Awareness
Circle of Sound Voice Education views singing as a dynamic way of knowing ourselves and as a psycho-spiritual form of being musical. "Knowing ourselves" simply means the ability to listen to our bodies and recognize our true feelings in a state of awareness. A psycho-spiritual form of being musical can be described as the practice of awareness—awareness of "self" and "other" as a unified and interconnected whole. The concept of interconnectedness is described by Jewish theologian Martin Buber as "I and Thou"[7] and by Zen Master Thich Nhat Hanh as "Interbeing."[8] The chapter on Awareness includes a reflection on the beginning of my own contemplative journey entitled "Learning to Breathe Again," plus an interview led by my colleague Dr. Lori Dolloff at the University of Toronto Faculty of Music. In this section of the book, Bill Perison and I discuss the circumstances that brought our contemplative and musical worlds together in a most fruitful way.

The Second Foundation: Mindfulness
The instructional approach in *Circle of Sound Voice Education* is based on a core practice of carefully sequenced breathing, movement, and vocalization exercises designed to calm, center, and focus the singer. In our extensive chapter on mindfulness we demonstrate the exercises in sequence. We have included graphics and music notation for the singer, coach, and accompanist. We describe the important distinctions between breathing and *conscious* breathing, movement and *intentional* movement, and vocalization and *in-formed* vocalization.

Through conscious breathing, the singer learns to work in the present moment, free of the fear and anxiety of the past or the future. These conscious breathing exercises are designed to encourage the singer to concentrate on and *intentionalize* inhalation, move naturally and continuously with the breath, and "let go" of the tonal outcome.

As students are guided through a sequenced series of repeated breathing, movement, and vocalization exercises, they learn to calm, concentrate, and center the mind and body. From the calm and centered Self, students begin to trust and appreciate the sacred nature of the singing experience as a safe and quiet place. As singers start to recognize their own inner processes physically and emotionally, they begin to concentrate quietly and listen deeply. The singer learns to dwell in the present moment, free of past failures or future anxieties.

The Third Foundation: Deep Listening
Circle of Sound Voice Education emphasizes a quality of singing unattached to a prescribed vocal outcome or "tone idyll." *Circle of Sound* is not a prescription or an exercise in sounding perfect or sounding like "this one or that one." The quality of the breath (respiration) informs the quality of the vocalization (phonation). When the singer practices conscious breathing, she comes into the present moment fully aware of herself in the here and the now, free from unnecessary thoughts and distractions.

Using musical examples from Doreen Rao's *Choral Music Experience* series, the chapter on deep listening in rehearsal and performance expands and illustrates the core practice to include rehearsal applications in the musical context of traditional and contemporary solo and unison songs.

Opening the Circle

The Fourth Foundation: Well-Being

Circle of Sound Voice Education views singing as a contemplative and inclusive practice—a way of recognizing ourselves and others in relation to the artistic, social, and intellectual phenomenon of song and song traditions. Metaphorically, as well as physically, singing is a form of movement, movement is a form of breath, breath is a form of life, and life is a form of spirit. In Latin, the word for breath, "spirare," means spirit. *Conscious breathing* (spirit) and *intentional movement* (life) sew together the mind and body—through singing.

To illuminate the importance of the foundation of well-being, we provide a summary of research about singing and education, and share case study excerpts about the *Circle of Sound* core practice. The case studies were submitted to us by conductors, singers, and teachers in the fields of voice performance and choral music education. They provide first-hand experiences about the effectiveness of using *Circle of Sound Voice Education* in a variety of teaching contexts.

In the chapter entitled "Closing the Circle," we've broadly summarized key concepts of *Circle of Sound* for music education today and have provided an introduction to t'ai chi movement practice with Bill Perison.

Summary

As we begin to understand singing as a form of mindful breathing, well-being, deep listening, and awareness, we can also begin to appreciate the multidimensional nature of singing as a life enriching and healing musical experience. This inclusive voice education practice embraces the diversity of cross-cultural vocal traditions and practices rooted in the twenty-first century realities of modern life. In the spirit of Rumi's poem quoted earlier, "Where Everything is Music," we invite you to replace words with conscious breathing, "open the window in the center of your chest" through intentional body movement, and "let the spirits fly in and out" through the beauty and freedom of a singing voice free from fear and anxiety.

"Perfection is not the issue in the circle. Practice is enough."
—Christina Baldwin
from Calling the Circle

Chapter 2
The First Foundation: Awareness

Circle of Sound Voice Education combines the traditional bel canto techniques of singing with breathing meditation practices and *taijiquan* movement forms. Through a systematic series of breathing, movement, and vocal exercises carefully adapted from these selected contemplative practices, the student learns to "come home" to the breath as a primary source of vocal understanding and musical insight.

Combining both traditional and alternative teaching strategies, the *Circle of Sound* practice facilitates a safe and encouraging environment that allows for a certain resonance and synergy to occur in a relatively brief period of time. When, for example, a student learns to breathe consciously and let go of the fear and anxiety associated with so-called "flawless technique," she begins to recognize the "universe within"—the power of Self as the primary source of musical understanding. As she learns to sing in an emotionally and spiritually conscious manner, the musical experience delivers both artistic and therapeutic rewards to her and the world around her.

In this quiet and concentrated environment, the teacher serves as a trusted guide, role model, mentor, and coach. The vocal coach guides the student to reflect on both the physical and emotional feelings associated with her vocalism. In the voice studio, rehearsal room, or concert hall, the student will learn to return "home" regularly to the conscious breathing and intentional movement practices that connect her to her body, the music, and the energy sources around her.

The repeated use of this contemplative approach to singing creates calm and the ability to listen deeply. The student recognizes *where* she is, and concentrates on *what* she is doing and *who* she is doing it with. The student's body will begin to "talk back" to her, and as her breathing and movement practice improves, she will begin to "observe" herself and listen deeply with calm, concentration, and understanding.

From the Past, Toward the Future

The evolution of the *Circle of Sound* approach to voice education began in the context of my growing friendship with Bill Perison. Bill was my *taijiquan* teacher. As we began to work, I learned that Bill had a degree in music education. He had always wanted to sing, so I started teaching him voice in exchange for lessons in *taijiquan*. As our friendship developed, I realized that Bill's university musical experiences in trumpet performance had left him with a good deal of fear and anxiety associated with performing. His singing voice was very restricted and he was unable to phonate without "clutching" or holding on to the tone. This fear-based reaction to singing greatly minimized the size and quality of his singing tone.

To ease the tension of trying to sing, Bill intuitively began moving around the room as he vocalized. In fact, he began to use movement forms extracted from his favorite parts of *taijiquan*. As he moved gracefully and easily through the *taijiquan* forms, his breath was naturally activated and he was able to

The First Foundation

connect the breath to his singing tone without trying. From the safe and comfortable place of his *taijiquan* movements, Bill's breath activated the kind of vocal tone that transformed his singing voice within minutes from a small and restricted tenor sounding tone quality to a full bodied and resonant bass baritone voice.

This amazing discovery was a gift to both of us. It was the beginning of what we later came to call the *Circle of Sound*. It was the beginning of Bill's true and resonant baritone voice, and it was the beginning of our six-year collaboration in developing this exciting contemplative approach to voice education.

My association with Bill Perison would prove to be pivotal to the creation and authoring of the *Circle of Sound Voice Education*. Yet, it was several years after Bill's vocal breakthrough that we had an epiphany about how to connect our two seemingly different worlds to create a contemplative approach to singing. It wasn't until I agreed to meet another friend of mine on the Canadian west coast for a meditation retreat that I found myself journeying from the past toward the future.

So many people have asked me how this connection between vocal performance, meditation, and the martial arts began for me. The following story tells it all.

Learning to Breathe Again!

Every singer knows how to breathe, right? Singers are taught how to breathe at their first singing lesson. So when my friend Merle invited me to join her on a trip to Vancouver Island's remote northeastern coast to learn breathing meditation, I chuckled and reminded her arrogantly that I was a "singer," and "singers know how to breathe"—that's what we do! Because Merle was coming all the way from South Africa to attend this meditation retreat, I agreed to join her strictly as a gesture of friendship.

On our way to Vancouver Island, I learned that the "breathing teacher" Joan Halifax was an anthropologist and wilderness guide. The irony of an experienced teacher of singing (me!) flying two thousand miles across the continent to study breathing technique with an unknown anthropologist and wilderness guide had to be accepted with midlife-crisis humor.

Enjoying the natural beauty of northern Vancouver Island, we met our teacher Joan Halifax. With a "suspect" attitude worn in style by so many members of the academic community, I joined Merle for our first meditation lesson. Cross-legged and in a quietly uncomfortable sitting position, only my previous two years of *taijiquan* practice with Bill Perison saved me from stomping out. With the kind of quick judgment that comes best from a lifetime of technical achievement, I thought "this is not the kind of breathing singers know."

Our meditation teacher taught us the basics of what she called mindfulness practice, a non-sectarian form of conscious breathing in the tradition of Vietnamese Zen master the Venerable Thich Nhat Hanh. Thay (the Vietnamese word for teacher) is famous for "correcting" Descartes's famous *cogito ergo sum* ("I think, therefore I am") to the Zen version "I think, therefore I am not." It was difficult for me to understand the apparent contradiction between being "mindful" as in "thinking," and being "mindful" as in "breathing and not thinking." At first, I was unable to make the connection between breathing mindfully and dwelling in awareness.

By the third meditation lesson of the week, I was able to keep my mind on my breath. In a short period of time, my breathing became deep and gentle. As my breathing quieted, my mind and body also became peaceful. Usually my mind is doing one thing and my body is doing another. In just a few minutes of conscious breathing meditation, my body and mind came back together and became whole again. By concentrating on my breathing, I began to think less, feel refreshed, and come back to myself in the present moment.

The First Foundation

As I practiced conscious breathing throughout the week, I realized that I was learning to breathe again! I developed what my teacher called "a beginner's mind," a place of "not knowing" where I could stop, feel calm, recognize where I was, concentrate fully, and understand more deeply. As my meditation practice developed, I began to feel a difference in my teaching and performing. Since then, the benefits of mindfulness breathing have had a profound effect on my teaching and connecting.

Doreen Rao and Bill Perison in Conversation with Lori Dolloff

Led by Dr. Lori Dolloff, associate professor and coordinator of music education at the University of Toronto, the following interview with Doreen Rao and Bill Perison took place in August 1999 at the University's Faculty of Music.

Lori Dolloff:
Doreen and Bill, I have really enjoyed working with you at this year's *Choral Music Experience* Institute for Choral Teacher Education in Chicago. I found that *Circle of Sound* has influenced my own teaching practice—both as a singer and as a choral conductor. Doreen, having watched your work since the early 1980s, I have seen you grow immensely. I am wondering about the growth and development of this new voice education practice.

Doreen Rao:
I think that my work as a singer, conductor, and teacher has changed enormously, especially in the past four years. These changes came about first through my own healing work, which began with Bill Perison through the martial arts movement practice of *taijiquan*. *Taijiquan* influenced me tremendously. To practice this martial arts form, I had to "stop," "root down," and find my "center of intention." The ability to stop and root down into the earth made an amazing difference in how I felt about my own space, my body, and my ability to move in time and space. The *taijiquan* practice put me in touch with my breath center in a way that I found absolutely remarkable. From the time of my first lesson, Bill continued to teach me until he moved to Vancouver Island two years later. During the same period, I started teaching Bill voice lessons. It was quite by accident that we realized there was a close connection between the martial arts movement forms of *taijiquan* and traditional voice-teaching techniques.

Bill Perison:
After we met, Doreen began experimenting with the use of *taijiquan* body movements in the context of her rehearsal warm-ups with her choirs. We had the students rooting down and relaxing at the beginning of each rehearsal. The warm-up movements seemed to have an immediate influence on the students. The sound of their singing became instantly more resonant and they began to focus quickly. The warm-up time taken at the beginning of the rehearsals paid off with great dividends.

DR:
I agree. While the *taijiquan* movements had a remarkable effect on the singing, I also felt that the quality of our communication improved. It was the quiet concentration that allowed the singers to learn so much more music and learn it more deeply. It was surprising to both of us that the *taijiquan* movement practice had such an immediate effect on such a large number of students who had little or no singing background.

LD:
During the early stages of your field testing, you were frequently working with very large groups. Can you talk about the number of students that you engaged in this way?

The First Foundation

DR:
Let's take for example the North York Board of Education Choral Project in Toronto, Canada's largest school board. This longitudinal research and professional development project in the schools involved teachers, classroom choirs, selected school choirs, and eventually an auditioned festival choir chosen from across the Board of Education. There were sometimes up to 200 and 300 students singing in a project. The auditioned festival choir numbered around 100 singers. I used the conscious breathing and intentional movement practices with the teachers, the classroom choirs, and the auditioned choirs. We found the results to be significant in all these varied contexts.

In large urban festival settings throughout the United States and Canada, I will often meet 300 students or more. These situations require a tremendous amount of energy and expertise to engage the students, help them focus, and feel comfortable and joyful with the singing experience. The breathing and movement practice seems to quiet everyone instantly from the inside out. Similarly, with smaller groups of 100 or less auditioned students, the benefits are stunning. The quality of the singing tone seems to be organically unified—so free and so resonant.

LD:
How would you respond to a teacher that said "I could never get my kids to do that?"

DR:
I think any practice, technique, or tradition has to be comfortable and appealing to the people who use it. I think the task is to "do it"—to experience the practice, to "practice the practice." That's what I hope *Circle of Sound Voice Education* will do. It can guide teachers and singers in the breathing, movement, and vocalization practice. I would encourage the teacher who said "I could never get my kids to do that" to practice the breathing and movement exercises and work only from the personal perspective of her own body and her own experience.

LD:
Bill, what kind of response do you see from the students that are participating in this practice?

BP:
I find that they really enjoy it. They enjoy the opportunity to move. They connect with themselves and with one another. When we play around with "rooting down," they are amazed at how strong they can be. And they enjoy the breathing. They're always willing participants.

DR:
As Bill mentioned, the "rooting down" connects us to ourselves and to one another. Not unlike teachers and conductors, students today are moving too fast. *Taijiquan* movement helps us to slow down and actually learn to be with ourselves in our own spaces. Children and adults alike really respond immediately to that "quiet connection." It feels good. But it's not always easy at first. Some of us find it hard to stop and slow down. Most people, however, develop a sense of trust in that quiet space. I think the element of trust and the feeling of quiet within directly influences the way we learn.

LD:
You've connected t'ai chi movement practice to your singing practice. Bill, I'm wondering if you can describe your own vocal development?

BP:
As I was working with Doreen, teaching her *taijiquan*, we began experimenting with movement, breathing, and singing. As Doreen coached my vocalization, I intuitively began using elements of the t'ai chi form as I sang. As I "moved" during the vocal exercises, I began to trust the connection between the movement forms and the singing experience. In an astounding all-at-once moment that I'll never forget, I released my voice to a full-throated resonance that startled both Doreen and me. In the safety and "easiness" of the movement and breath space, I had let go of "holding" and "analyzing" the tone. My throat just opened up. My voice went

The First Foundation

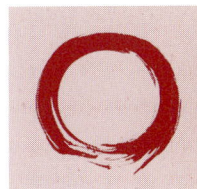

from a kind of tentative high tenor to what Doreen called a "confident bass baritone." The resonance I felt was phenomenal and empowering.

DR:
I think that Bill's experience was very profound. I remember that we were able to work from the movement of t'ai chi directly into his vocalism. And because he was familiar and comfortable with the *taijiquan* practice, he could use those familiar movements as a container for the voice. He was able to "let go" of the psychological and physical restrictions that had been blocking his true voice.

Bill could do the *taijiquan* movements in the context of his *taijiquan* practice, but as he started singing, he would stop moving. He would actually stop breathing. And because there was so much fear and anxiety associated with performing in the past, he was unconsciously "holding" his body and breath, restricting any possibility of tonal resonance. When Bill began to sing from the breath and movement space, his voice "found itself." His singing transformed from a tentative, falsetto-like sound, to a resonant and assured full-bodied tone. Bill's new voice developed within minutes of this breath and movement connection.

BP:
I remember feeling so comfortable with the movements. I followed the *taijiquan* form and found my voice-in-the-movement. As I followed the movement, the voice was there.

DR:
Bill found his voice naturally and organically, directly from the breath and movement practice. Of course the movement encouraged the breath. The movement is a manifestation of breath, just as singing is a manifestation of movement.

LD:
Doreen, I know you've been using this practice with beginning-level singers, with children, and also with university voice majors who have been singing for a long time. Do you see the same kind of results with accomplished adult singers as you have had with children and beginning singers?

DR:
This approach to singing has been field-tested formally in a wide variety of settings. We've been using it with university choirs and voice students. It's been used in large urban choral festival settings with hundreds of young students. For example, I have been using it with Dianne Berkun's Brooklyn Youth Choir's school singing projects in New York, and with the North York Board of Education Choral Projects in Toronto. As you know, it is also being used in the conducting courses I teach.

Like any teaching approach, *Circle of Sound* must be adapted with sensitivity to meet the needs of each individual singer and each unique ensemble. Young choirs, children's choirs, and beginning-level amateur choirs enthusiastically jump into this practice without hesitation. The results are immediate and significant. These groups generally work in a more intuitive manner. At the high school and university levels of instruction, I generally use an adaptation of the approach. As the students sense the benefits of the practice, I introduce more and more of the exercises as required. I think that there is a common thread that runs through all of these contexts. Through breathing and movement, all singers can move away from fear and anxiety into a quiet, trusting space that is encouraged and supported by the practice of conscious breathing and intentional movement.

LD:
One of the elements of the *Circle of Sound* core practice is breathing. Of course, breathing is the "inspiration" for all of singing, so how did you get then, from the movement of t'ai chi, into the breathing practice, then into vocalization?

The First Foundation

DR:
Well, the breathing practice for me began quite apart from my work in the martial arts. During the summer months, I had the opportunity to study with anthropologist and Zen teacher, Joan Halifax. On a beautiful island setting in British Columbia, Joan taught the practice of mindfulness meditation. Mindfulness is a conscious-breathing approach to meditation. While mindfulness is a secular or non-sectarian practice, the exercises are rooted in Mahayana or "engaged" Buddhism, brought to the West in this context by Vietnamese peace activist and Zen master Thich Nhat Hanh.

As I learned mindfulness, I remember thinking that conscious breathing held tremendous potential for voice education specifically and music performance generally. I started to explore the use of mindfulness breathing in my own singing and with my choirs in their warm-ups. Then I discovered that the conscious breathing exercises were particularly beneficial when I connected them to the *taijiquan* movement exercises I'd experimented with earlier. When I connected conscious breathing and t'ai chi movement, I was stunned at the difference in vocal tone, and the difference again in people's ability to feel comfortable with their own bodies.

BP:
I remember when Doreen first shared the conscious breathing practice with me. It was the same day we had that momentous voice lesson—the lesson in which she combined the breathing as an integral part of *taijiquan* movement. It was a unique application of both the breathing and movement practices. Consciously breathing-in and breathing-out with the thought of releasing the tone to the out-breath, I remember that first-time connection. My breathing became a very conscious and active thing. Breathing-out was more of a relaxed not-so-active event in the movement.

DR:
Bill, you stopped trying to "control" the tone.

BP:
Right. Around that same time we began experimenting with linking the conscious breathing exercises and the *taijiquan* movements with traditional vocalizations. As we began weaving together the alternative breathing and movement practices with the traditional vocal exercises, we developed the three-part core practice that we are sharing for the first time in text form.

DR:
I think it was after I began to work in breathing meditation, and after we began to connect what we knew about *taijiquan* movement practice with what I knew about breathing and voice pedagogy, that the *Circle of Sound* paradigm actually started to come together. We went from the original practice of *taijiquan* form to what we call "intentional movement," and from the original practice of mindfulness meditation to what we call "conscious breathing," and from the original practice of bel canto vocal technique to what we call "in-formed vocalization." These are the three core components of *Circle of Sound Voice Education*.

LD:
How would you characterize the difference then between bel canto technique and the *Circle of Sound* vocalization exercises you were talking about right now?

DR:
Circle of Sound combines both traditional and alternative techniques in voice education as a way of freeing the body of the fear and anxiety associated with concert performance. Bel canto singing technique is a particular kind of vocal tone. In the field of classical music and music education, bel canto is the predominant method of voice production. Generally speaking, bel canto is often taught from a "sound ideal"—the student is encouraged to produce a particular kind of tone, a tone the teacher or conductor has in mind for each student or each choir. In some studios, the "sound ideal" would be whatever sound the teacher thought was the "real" or "true" voice of the singer or choir.

The First Foundation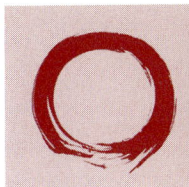

Voice education is usually a practice-based form of instruction that includes the use of vocalizations and other warm-up exercises to access tone. Most vocalizations focus directly on the tone quality itself. Perhaps the distinguishing feature of the *Circle of Sound* approach to singing has to do with the primary focus on the quality of the respiration rather than the quality of the tone itself. In this approach, the tone is not "placed" or "controlled." If the breath is informed skillfully, the quality of the tone will follow in kind. In *Circle of Sound*, the singing voice is thought of as a physical manifestation of the whole person. The voice is who we are when we sing.

This approach does not focus on the voice alone—but on the *origins* of vocalization—the *quality* of the breath and the *feeling* of the movement. This focus takes us organically to the *source* of singing—it doesn't treat the symptoms. The intentional-movement forms connect the breath to the tone, activating the breath in very specific and systematic ways, so the singer can "let go" of the tone. Obviously, the singer has a particular artistic quality or a musical idea in mind, but with this kind of approach to breathing through movement, that tone can take on whatever quality the singer makes conscious through breathing.

LD:
And do you find that singers who have been studying for a long time find this quality of vocalization a "letting go" experience when they learn to use this practice?

DR:
We've had some remarkable results, Lori. This past summer we worked with some very accomplished professional singers, and by the fourth day of instruction, some of the singers in the group had profound and life-changing experiences. Many singers said that it was the very first time they heard themselves. They told us they didn't feel like their singing was like going through a checklist of things that they had to do, such as manipulate, make, control, or manage the voice. They said that the breathing and movement practice had allowed the voice to "sing itself."

We heard incredible changes in resonance. We heard qualities and colors that sent chills down our spines. The deep and conscious breathing through movement opened the throat so entirely that the singers did not find it necessary to approach brighter vowel sounds sung on high pitches through the use of vowel modification. Instead of singing a high tone on a modified open vowel, the high pitches were sung on the original unmodified bright vowels with an absolutely chillingly beautiful result. Instead of being "manipulated," these tones were ringing and real—perhaps this is what voice pedagogues call the "true voice." The singers felt they had found their "own" voices, not the voices of the "tone ideal," not the voices that their teachers prescribed, but a natural and easy resonance, the voices that "felt good" to them.

LD:
You've mentioned using the *Circle of Sound* practice with beginning level singers and also with professional singers. What are the other contexts in which you've used the practice?

DR:
As I have mentioned, in the past three years I've had the opportunity to field test *Circle of Sound* in the context of large choral festivals from 200 up to 1,000 singers, where I've adapted some of the core practices to use *en masse*. In these large festival contexts, I've found that the level of concentration and the quality of performance improved enormously.

I remember working with Dianne Berkun and her Brooklyn Youth Chorus (BYC). The BYC hosted a school performance program for urban New York school choirs called "Let the Children Sing New York!" These children came from a wide variety of backgrounds. Many had never sung a day in their lives. They sat spread out over an enormous auditorium in Brooklyn, and when I started the breathing and movement practice the teachers thought "Oh no, she's not going to try to do that, is she?" No one had any expectation that these children could do anything quietly, much less with artistry and concentration. Within the first ten minutes, the rehearsal went from total chaos to quiet concentration. We all had a

 # The First Foundation

profound and life-changing experience together with those New York teachers and their students. In three days, the large festival choir literally transformed from a group of predominantly hyperactive non-singers to an extraordinarily focused and accomplished choral ensemble of young singers.

Also, throughout the past several summers, as I've used *Circle of Sound* with professional singers, high school singers and university students, I found that the *Circle of Sound* approach has been successful in all these varied contexts. I think the bottom line is that you teach what it is you want to learn, and you need to practice what you teach. It's as simple as that. I practice conscious breathing so I can listen deeply to my students and their singing, and so I can teach my students to listen deeply to me, to themselves, and to others around them. *Circle of Sound* is now being used by many of my teaching colleagues. I think they are finding it useful to achieve deep listening and concentration in rehearsals and in classrooms.

Chapter 3
The Second Foundation: Mindfulness
Circle of Sound Core Practice

In his popular book *Peace Is Every Step*, Zen Master Thich Nhat Hanh describes mindfulness as a way of being fully present in each breath, in each step. "When we breathe consciously we recover ourselves completely and encounter life in the present moment."[1] The practice of mindfulness through conscious breathing teaches us to *calm* the body and the mind, *recognize* where we are and whom we are with, *concentrate* fully, and *understand* things more deeply.

Through mindfulness, qualities of focus and concentration, attitude and efficiency, and a deeper sense of enjoyment are most always present. You can "feel" the focus. You can "hear" the quiet. Mindfulness breathing is the essence and the foundation of this contemplative approach to voice education.

Circle of Sound Core Practice

Circle of Sound Voice Education begins with a simple series of breathing, movement, and vocal exercises practiced at the beginning of each lesson or rehearsal. These core practice exercises may be used before, or in place of, standard vocal warm-ups. It is essential to use these exercises systematically at the beginning of each meeting so both the students and the teacher can establish a centered and productive working relationship that will benefit the quality of teaching and learning.

As a coach, the teacher guides the student's breathing, movement, and vocalization practice until the student can skillfully and independently feel the fluid and uninterrupted connection with her breath and her body as a primary source of vocal resonance. This process requires that the teacher and the student be fully present in the here and the now, able to let go of past experiences and future expectations. In short, this is the practice of mindfulness.

Each lesson or rehearsal should start diligently with the core practice exercises outlined in this chapter. The exercises encourage the calm of conscious breathing, the connection of conscious breathing to intentional body movement, and the natural progression of breath to movement to vocalization. The core practice is used at the start of each meeting, the benefit of inner quiet, calm, and deep concentration will consistently bring participants into the "present moment" or "mindfulness."

Over time, as the singer's mindfulness deepens, she will develop a quiet confidence, a deep concentration, and a heightened awareness. Mindfulness will lead her beyond the fear and anxiety of technical challenges into a more joyful and confident singing practice.

It is important to consider the difference in quality between breathing and *conscious breathing*, between movement and *intentional movement*, and between vocalizing and *in-formed vocalizing*. These qualities can be understood as the difference between *reflexive* and *reflective*, *mindless* and *mindful*, *thoughtless* and *thoughtful* actions.

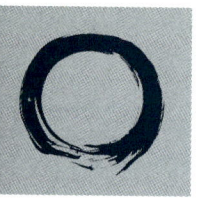

The Second Foundation

Consciousness and intention inform the singing voice. When the singer is fully present in each of the breathing, movement, and vocalization exercises, the singing voice gains a "personal presence"—a natural beauty that develops organically from a deep connection with the "inner voice." This quality of singing experience is a form of life lived in consonance with one's own deepest nature and with the ways of the natural world.[2]

Core Practice Exercises

The core practice exercises begin with conscious-breathing extended into a combination of conscious-breathing and intentional-movement exercises, extended into a combination of conscious-breathing, intentional-movement, and in-formed vocalization exercises.

The use of stretching exercises can also help prepare the body and mind for singing. A sequenced series of stretching exercises is developed in Chapter 6 by Bill Perison. These recommended stretching exercises can be used at the beginning of the warm-ups to enhance the *Circle of Sound* core practice of breathing, movement, and vocalization exercises. The following "Circle Progression" diagram illustrates how the core practices exercises are sequenced and interdependent.

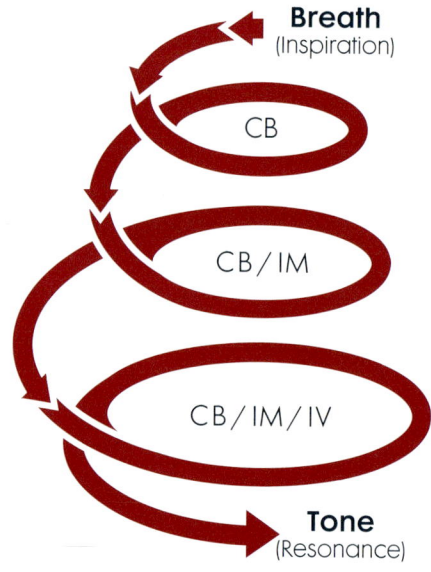

Circle Progression: The Core Practice

Before we illustrate and guide the *Circle of Sound* core practice, we will first introduce and briefly discuss each of the constituent elements of *Circle of Sound Voice Education*. These elements include: conscious breathing, intentional movement, and in-formed vocalization. We will discuss the origin of each element, followed by a description of the evolution of these elements as they came to form the *Circle of Sound Voice Education* core practice. The core practice exercises begin on page 26.

Conscious Breathing

Conscious breathing can be described as a form of mindfulness. Mindfulness can become an integral part of daily teaching and performing work. At all levels of instruction, from school children to accomplished singers and distinguished conductors, we have found that mindfulness makes a profound difference in the way teachers teach and in the way students learn. We use the same sequence of breathing exercises for all levels of learning, including children and adults, novices and experts.

When we practice conscious breathing, our thinking will slow down. Most of us think too much! We often say to our singers "breathe more, think less." Breathing is a way of developing attention, nourishing awareness, and being present in every moment.

Conscious breathing can be practiced regularly in each rehearsal or lesson to connect our minds to our bodies. Anthropologist and Zen teacher Joan Halifax Roshi says, "our breathing is a thread sewing together mind, body, and the world."[3] As we breathe-in, we say to ourselves, "Breathing-in, I know that I am breathing-in." As we breathe-out, we say, "Breathing-out, I know that I am breathing-out." The goal is simply to recognize our in-breath as an in-breath and our out-breath as an out-breath.

The Second Foundation

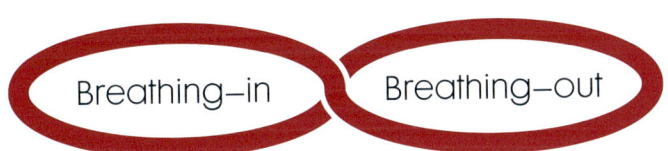

As we continue breathing-in and breathing-out, we can use just two words: "In"—"Out." This guiding technique helps keep our minds on our breath. As we practice routinely, we calm our bodies and our minds. We become peaceful. When we breathe consciously, we recover our true selves and learn to concentrate deeply.

As we practice conscious breathing, we can develop deep awareness. We are able to observe our body posture and our body movements. In this breathing practice, we don't have to "control" our breathing. Whether our in-breath is long or short, deep or slow, we just breathe naturally. When we do this, we notice our abdomen rising and falling with each breath. Our breathing becomes slower and deeper by itself. As we continue breathing-in and breathing-out, we become calmer and more at ease. We stop struggling, we release our anxieties, and we are able to smile to ourselves.

We know there are more than three hundred muscles in our face, and when we "breathe-in smiling," these muscles relax. Some teachers call "breathing-in smiling" mouth yoga.

The regular practice of conscious breathing helps us to stop, calm ourselves, recognize where we are and what we're doing. It helps us to concentrate and understand. In just a few minutes of quiet, gentle breathing, we feel refreshed and nourished. The following breathing poem can be used to help guide our breathing until words are no longer necessary.

Breathing-in.
Breathing-out.
Key words: In. Out.

Breathing-in deeply.
Breathing-out slowly.
Key words: Deep. Slow.

Breathing-in calmly.
Breathing-out with ease.
Key words: Calm. Ease.

Breathing-in smiling.
Breathing-out release.
Key words: Smile. Release.

With this simple conscious-breathing exercise, we can develop a mindfulness *of* our body *in* the body, and a mindfulness *of* the music *in* the music. As we breathe-in, we learn to be fully present with things just as they are, not as they were in the past, and not as we think we want them to be in the future. Mindfulness breathing helps us to know ourselves and the world around us. It is a technique for centering the "inner voice," connecting with the "outer voice," and listening deeply. The conscious breathing exercises begin on page 26.

Circle of Sound Voice Education • 17

The Second Foundation

Intentional Movement

The kind of voice education that helps our students develop inner strength and confidence, deep listening ability, and body awareness is the kind of voice education that benefits the students' health and well-being.

If we think of singing as a soundful manifestation of body, mind, and spirit, and if we view the singing voice as a natural extension of body movement, we are ethically bound to consider organic approaches to voice education that will provide an inclusive foundation for the physical, mental, and spiritual well-being of the singer. *Circle of Sound Voice Education* focuses on the sources of singing over the symptoms of sounding, the health and wellness of the singer over the technically flawless "performance-at-any-cost," and the soulful, authentic voice over the perfect "tone idyll."

Movement and body work in voice education is by no means a new idea. There are many influential schools of thought and practice that have contributed to the quality of vocal performance and singing instruction as we know it today. Whatever movement practice a singer adopts, it is crucially important that the practice is consciously integrated into the vocalism.

We have developed a movement practice adapted from *taijiquan* (t'ai chi ch'uan) over the benefits of other excellent approaches because of its characteristics of continuousness and connectedness in time and space. Defined as a form of "body knowing," *taijiquan* is an ancient martial art with an emphasis on internal strength, deep awareness, and the balance of yin (ease) and yang (active).

We view the use of *taijiquan* for singers as having a number of unique and profound benefits related to the continuous movement and interdependent workings of the vocal apparatus. For performing and teaching, *taijiquan* practice helps to develop both physical and mental strength. The use of sequentially developed movement patterns are intended to slow and soften, strengthen and balance, align, root, and center the body.

This personal narrative tells one story:

> In my own practice of *taijiquan*, I developed a new kind of strength that was notably different from what I had previously understood as "strength." As I practiced rooting, centering, and the beginning movement forms with my teacher, my fast-paced manner shifted from terribly intense to more relaxed, from frenetically fast to somewhat slower, and from loud to a little bit softer. Though it was difficult at the start, I gradually and gratefully came to accept the benefits of this movement practice. My colleagues and my students noticed the difference.
>
> As my body began to enjoy the strength and gentleness of these movement forms, my mind seemed to slow and soften. I was more aware of my Self and the world around me. My daily actions, teaching, and performing were more considered and purposeful. I forgot less and focused more. My singing and conducting began to feel natural, organic, and really authentic. My teaching took on an interactive integrity as I learned to listen deeply to others without "needing to fill the spaces" with my own nervous and unnecessary thoughts.
>
> The most significant change I experienced from the *taijiquan* movement forms was the change in my ability to listen and diagnose my own singing and the singing of my choirs. While I have always been a fairly astute diagnostician, I was unprepared for the perceptual benefits that grew from a movement practice that improved my listening ability so dramatically. Deep listening is the basis for beautiful singing. This very skillful kind of "singing as listening" grew slowly and organically from the wisdom of my body.

The Second Foundation

While the *Circle of Sound* practice of intentional movement is developed and informed by the martial art of *taijiquan*, we carefully adapted the essence of the movement qualities from the traditional forms and shaped these into abbreviated and vocally related movements for the benefit of voice education. The intentional movement exercises begin on page 28.

In-formed Vocalization

In *Circle of Sound Voice Education*, we actively integrate the conscious-breathing and intentional-movement exercises into the vocalizations. As you will notice later in this text, the three constituent elements of the core practice are exercised interdependently. *Circle of Sound* embodies a holistic integration of conscious breathing and intentional movement as interdependent sources of singing.

As an introduction to the discussion of in-formed vocalization, it is important to address the sustaining value of traditional bel canto technique in singing. The consideration of new ideas and alternative possibilities for voice education does not require us to limit our thinking to any one set of principles or practices. As members of a culturally diverse society, it is easy for us to understand the necessity for a pluralistic account of singing and voice education.

There is so much about singing that is unseen. We can understand why vocal science has spent such vast amounts of time and attention on experimental research. Under microscopes and x-rays, exploratory surgery and computer prototypes, voice scientists and curious practitioners alike marvel at the complexity of the human voice. With the exception of the gross thoracic muscle movements associated with breathing, however, all vocal actions are invisible. And because the singer's ability to hear the sound of her own singing voice is developed primarily from the kinesthetic sense impression of the tone (feeling the tone), developing singers are particularly reliant on their teachers to tell them how to sing.

Traditional eighteenth-century Italian bel canto emphasizes the beauty and melodic quality of singing. Historical and contemporary debate surrounds the tradition of bel canto, particularly as an exclusive method in relation to the dynamic challenges of multicultural repertoire.

However, most singing schools and voice pedagogues agree on the acoustical description of the singing voice as an instrument consisting of a power supply (the lungs), an oscillator (the vocal folds), and a resonator (the larynx, pharynx, and mouth). The larynx, pharynx, and mouth together constitute what is called the vocal tract, which serves as a resonance chamber for singing. The shape of the vocal tract (how large or small, wide or long) is determined by the articulators: the lips, jaw, tongue, and the larynx. As the breath moves the articulators, the larynx lengthens, the pharynx widens, and the soft palate rises. From this acoustical description of the vocal tract, it may be possible to envision the "circle within" as an appropriate symbol of the singing voice.

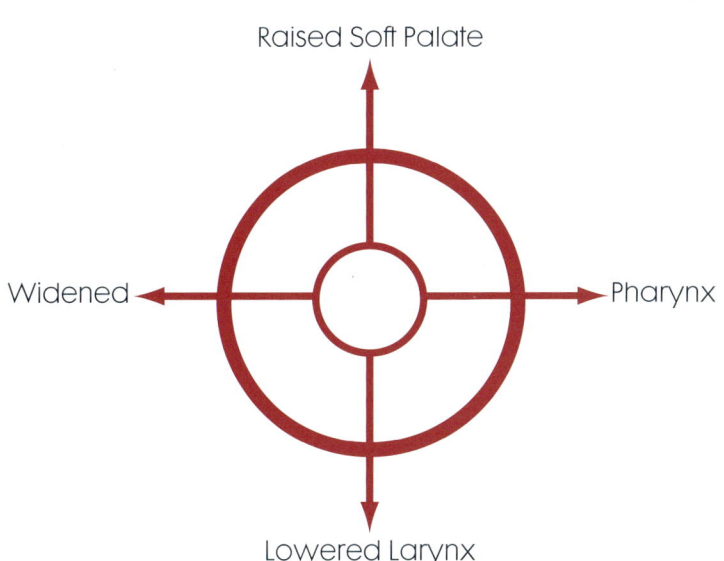

Imagining the vocal tract as the "circle within"

The Second Foundation

The unseen qualities of singing are both an advantage and a disadvantage for the singer. Because the singer cannot fully perceive the sound of his own voice once it leaves the lip opening and travels around the room and back into the ear canal, he is perhaps disadvantaged. But because the singer can also learn to rely on the feeling of the tone (the kinesthetic sense impression) as his primary avenue of listening, he has the advantage of the bone-conducted vibrations to inform his body and mind in singing. The acoustics of singing are a dynamic interrelationship of vibrations and energy, inside *and* outside the body.

Essentially, the singer enjoys a dual form of musical perception: one from the inside (he feels bone-conducted skull vibrations) and one from the outside (he hears interactive airborne vibrations). While singers rely more heavily upon the physical sensations of singing and less on the auditory feedback of sound waves, the singer can make use of both kinds of listening as a dynamic form of awareness.

When a singer practices systematic conscious breathing, she is practicing deep listening. When she practices deep listening, she sings with a naturally and organically informed tone that embodies her true nature. Different from the unfortunate struggles associated with trying to achieve a prescribed tone, or "tone idyll" (learning to sing from the outside-in), the singer who practices regular intentional body movement sings with a naturally and organically informed tone that manifests the authenticity of the "true voice" (learning to sing from the inside-out).

The core practice vocalizations are developed to concentrate on conscious breathing as a systematic approach to in-forming the singing tone. The purposefully slow and deep in-breath has a very active, intentional, yang-like quality that allows the out-breath to enjoy a free and easy yin-like quality. The breathing is continuous and circular and never stops moving. Throughout the vocalisation exercises, the student learns to maintain active awareness of her in-breath and is encouraged to "let go" of the tonal outcome.

The intelligent quality of the singer's inhalation ("inspiration") naturally in-forms the quality of the vocalism. Over a slow and purposeful in-breath, the inhalation can be informed variously in time by counting beats, evoking imagery, or by changing vowel formants. The vocalizations require the exercise of inhalation in "slow motion" as a purposeful and systematic element of the exercise. We call these periods of inhalation "breathing beats" or "breathing space." There is a strong focus on the quality of unsung time and space (breath preparation), and less focus on the thing sung (phonation).

In *Circle of Sound Voice Education*, our students are coached *not* to think. We teach Descartes in reverse: "I think, therefore I am not." In the same spirit, we also tell our students they already are what they want to become. Singers learn to "breathe-loud," "sing-soft," and replace thinking with breathing. One student recently said, "I now feel when I sing that I'm somehow connecting my entire body to the sound. The singing process now begins somewhere far deeper within me than it did before."[4] The in-formed vocalization exercises begin on page 34.

The Second Foundation

Circle of Sound Vocabulary

Circle of Sound is an "alternative" teaching approach evolved over time from lived musical and contemplative experiences. We have avoided using traditional vocabulary to describe these exercises and rehearsal techniques. While the mind can easily adapt to any kind of terminology, the body often refuses to forget less positive or affirming acts associated with the past.

The vocabulary we use to describe these "circle techniques" are words that *sound* and *feel* like the experience of singing itself rather than words borrowed from a technically driven or traditional pedagogy. *Circle* terms and phrases are introduced and discussed next.

Breathing Circle (Breath Circle)

The *breathing circle* is a dynamic image of both the metaphysical and physical spaces used for singing. It is the intentional act of shaping a large circle on the breath at the center of the body. The *breath circle* is a physical metaphor for the vocal tract, used to represent the unseen acoustical space of singing inside the body. We encourage the use of this term to support the singer's imagination of a "larger-than-life" resonance chamber. The act of shaping a *breath circle* in front of the body increases the singer's awareness of the active acoustical spaces around the singer. These outside-the-body acoustic spaces include the rehearsal or performance environments (the ceiling, the floors, the walls), the spaces created between members of the ensemble (the eye to eye human connection) and the natural human resonance created by the unique combination of ensemble singers. The *breath circle* can be used to stimulate and sustain respiratory action. It can be used to imagine the small micro movements and spaces within the vocal tract during phonation, making what is unseen and difficult to conceptualize easy to feel and understand. Breathing circles may be adapted in time and size to accommodate the particular musical requirements.

Breathing Space (Breath Space)

Breathing space is a dynamic image of the singer's "open throat" (the lowered larynx, lifted soft palate, and widened pharynx during phonation). The image of *breath space* is created by the movement metaphor of the *breath circle*. *Breathing space* includes all the spaces that inform the quality of the singer's voice and from which the singer may draw energy and support for singing. These include the spaces within the body (the vocal tract) and the spaces outside the body (the environmental spaces seen and unseen).

Listening Space (Deep Listening)

Listening space is the imaging of an open, circular space that develops from the calm of conscious breathing. When we breathe consciously and systematically we begin to listen deeply. Listening is a dynamic form of awareness that is the root of beautiful singing. When we breathe-in we create a "space for listening." Using the term *listening space* helps the singer focus her attention more on the qualities of breathing and listening and less on the act of sounding. *Listening space* provides the image of an acoustical environment for singing.

Singing Space

Breathing-in opens the acoustical spaces for listening. The term *singing space* is used to motivate the singer to imagine the circular, open shape of the vocal tract during phonation. *Singing space*, *listening space*, and *breathing space* "inter-are." These action-oriented metaphors are interdependent and can often be used interchangeably depending on the unique teaching context.

Breath Center

The *Circle of Sound* breath center is used interchangeably with the terms abdomen or *dantien*, the Chinese martial arts term for abdomen. The *breath center* is located approximately two inches below the navel and should not be confused with the stomach area which is higher up.

Circle of Sound Voice Education • 21

The Second Foundation

Breath Hand

Breath hand is the use of the hand to enact the *Circle of Sound* conscious breathing exercises. As the singer breathes-in, the *breath hand* circles down to and back up from the breath center to the area of the throat and face. Rounded and relaxed, this *breath hand* enactment parallels the process of air moving down (slow and low), the lowered larynx, the lifted palate and the tongue moving forward. The *breath hand* movement that parallels the open throat formation is an effective metaphor for the vocal tract movements during phonation.

Breath Hand

Breathing Beats

Breathing beats is a term used for the conscious inspiration (inhalation) for singing. The purposeful inhalation used over a prescribed length of time helps the singer to consciously prepare the breath slowly and deeply for singing. In the *Circle of Sound* core practice *breathing beats* are exercised over four counts preceding each vocalization. In the *Circle of Sound* extended practice *breathing beats* are exercised over varying counts determined by the unique musical context of the repertoire. For example, if a particular song has a four bar introduction of four beats per measure, the singer will use the last full measure of four beats as *breathing beats* in preparation for first vocal entrance. *Breathing beats* can be used before each new phrase is vocalized, and whenever there is a period of rest between phrases.

Circles-in-Time

Circles-in-time is an exercise closely related to breathing circles and breathing beats. It is the forming of multiple circles shaped in time and character to motivate the breath and imagine the open vocal tract throughout singing. The size and shape of *circles-in-time* will vary with each different musical context. *Circles-in-time* can include one large circle carried slowly over the full length of a long phrase. This particular circle variation is useful in supporting an even legato vocalism over an extended period. *Circles-in-time* can include a series of smaller circles carried on the beat or in the context of a particular rhythm pattern.

Circle Variations

Not all circles look alike. We can vary the shape of the *breath circle* to represent the uniquely expressive qualities and size of a melody, a phrase, or a particular interval required in a given musical context. *Breath circles* can be standard and round in shape, they can be large or small (micro or macro circles), they can be horizontal in quality, or they can be vertical and cylinder like. In the musical context of the repertoire, it is instructive to use circle variations as a way of helping singers imagine the open space of the vocal tract continuously.

Reading Circle

When singers work from the printed page, looking down at the music can adversely effect the quality of the vocalism. Teachers and conductors are forever asking their students to "look up" out of the score. Yet, looking up may not be enough to ensure the right acoustic space for singing. Using music stands adjusted at a fairly high position can free the singer's body and open the spaces around her. When singers must hold music, they can bring the printed page into the breath circle and think of the held score as an extension of the breath. By forming the breath circle with music held by both hands, the printed page becomes a part of the circle of sound.

The Second Foundation

Mindfulness Practice

A conscious state of dwelling in awareness, being fully present in the here and now, living in the present moment. A non-sectarian meditation practice introduced to the author by Zen Master Thich Naht Hanh, Vietnamese poet, teacher, and peace activist nominated for the Nobel Peace Prize by Martin Luther King, Jr. Mindfulness is practiced in diplomatic communities, in medical practices, and in educational environments throughout the world.

Conscious Breathing

A simple, non-sectarian breathing approach used by teachers, physicians, artists, diplomats, and therapists to sew together the body and the mind through systematic breathing-in and breathing-out. The practice of conscious breathing can guide us into a deeply conscious state of calm, concentration, recognition, and understanding. It is the first step to listening deeply and singing with non-fear.

Intentional Movement

A systematic form of body movement that is thoughtfully undertaken and guided by conscious breathing. Adapted by the authors from the martial art of *taijiquan* for practice by singers, conductors, and teachers, the quality of the movement forms is directly connected to the quality of conscious breathing. Intentional movement is a manifestation of breath in time and space, varied and adapted as required in musical context.

In-formed Vocalization

In-formed vocalization is the kind of singing that develops organically through the systematic processes of conscious breathing and intentional movement practice. Focusing more on the quality of inspiration (inhalation) and less on the manipulation of tonal outcome, this process allows the singer to "let go" of a preconceived "tone idyll" and learn to accept both her beautiful and not-so-beautiful tones. As the singer learns to trust her body and accept her limitations, she will begin to know her Self as a primary source for singing.

Breathing Loud, Singing Soft

The direction *breathe loud, sing soft* is used to encourage the singer to consciously activate the breath and "let go" of the tone. The terms "loud" and "soft" do not refer to the actual dynamic of sung pitch, but to the focused qualification of the singer's inspiration (inhalation) as the source of authentic tone and natural voice.

Circle Comments

In this contemplative singing practice, the quality of the in-breath (inspiration) is of fundamental importance. "Breathing-in" is an active, purposeful, and thoughtful action that combines with "breathing-out" or "singing out" as an organically informed extension of "breathing-in." When we concentrate on "breathing-in and breathing-out," we develop an awareness of the acoustical spaces for singing—the spaces within the body (the vocal tract) and the spaces outside the body (the room, the social dynamics, etc.). A deep awareness and acceptance of ourselves in relation to the acoustical spaces for singing, the vocal tract, and the concert hall contribute significantly to the creation of resonance. The vital qualities of resonance include both the kinesthetic sense impression of tone (the feeling of the tone in the body) as well as the stimulation of chemical changes associated with well-being and good health.

Now that we have explained the elements of the *Circle of Sound Voice Education* core practice and the *Circle* vocabulary, it is time to put explanation into action. You may want to tab the next section which contains:

1. *Circle of Sound*: A Teacher's Guide
2. Conscious Breathing Exercises
    (with short breathing poems and photographs)
3. Intentional Movement Exercises
    (with annotated photographs)
4. In-formed Vocalization Exercises
    (with musical notation and photographs)

The Second Foundation

Circle of Sound: A Teacher's Guide

As the student(s) arrive for rehearsals or lessons, it is essential that the teacher establish a purposeful atmosphere of calm and concentration. Verbal interactions with the student(s) and among the students in the rehearsal space should be limited to thoughtful questions or comments with the intention of making a mutually respectful human connection. The teacher's intentions should be made clear to the students, including the teacher's overall rehearsal or lesson goals, repertoire to be learned and musical expectations to be realized.

The energy of the environment should contribute to the contemplative nature of this quiet and concentrated exchange. This includes encouraging the students to limit or eliminate verbal interactions after they come through the door into the "quiet" space. If the teacher is already in a "contemplative space" when the students arrive, they will respond similarly.

In the studio or rehearsal room, the teacher can guide the conscious breathing exercises in a sitting or standing circle. If the group is large and the chairs or risers are stationary, a semicircle formation will suffice. In all settings, the teacher should demonstrate the exercises and practice with the students whenever it is possible.

1. *Circle of Sound* **conscious breathing** should begin quietly, without discussion. As the students enter the instructional environment and observe the teacher's inner quiet they will begin to quiet themselves without the aid of verbal interaction. If words are necessary, they should be brief and used in a quiet voice. The teacher's ability to create a sense of quiet purpose is the first step in helping the students to stop and calm their bodies and minds. As the students settle into their quiet breathing space, the teacher can begin to guide the conscious breathing exercises in sequence. (See Conscious Breathing Exercises, p. 26.)

Once the conscious breathing practice is established as routine, the role of the breathing guide can be assumed by a student apprentice guide who shows a readiness and interest in leading the exercises.

2. *Circle of Sound* **intentional movement** exercises can begin naturally from the end of the conscious breathing practice. If the students are in a sitting position, the teacher can invite the students to stand slowly on their in-breath. If the students are standing during the conscious breathing exercises, they can prepare for the movement exercises with the hands circling out slowly on their in-breath. At the beginning of the intentional movement exercises, the teacher should demonstrate the breath circle posture in preparation for the *breathing-in-moving* exercises. The breathing-in-moving circle moves from the large macro-circle on the in-breath to the smaller micro-circle then back out to the macro-circle during the out-breath. The movement works from a large circle outside and around the middle of the body into a smaller circle closer to the body's breath center (the region of the abdomen, slightly below the waist) then back out to the large circle.

It is important for teachers to note that this particular breathing-movement pattern *reverses* the traditional "breathing-in, moving-out, breathing-out, moving-in" patterns often associated with breathing for singing. The *Circle of Sound* intentional movement form is designed to help singers conceptualize the open vocal tract "circle inside" throughout vocalization by way of directing an "outside-the-body" movement pattern that mirrors the "inside-the-body" movement of the larynx, pharynx and soft palate. The "outside-the-body" circle movement involving the arms and the upper torso serves as a metaphor for the physiological processes taking place internally.

Circle of Sound intentional movement practice is always circular. While the breath and the breath-inspired movement exercises are interdependent and always connected, the teacher should carefully monitor the breathing activity of the students during the movement exercises. Sometimes a student

The Second Foundation

will inadvertently hold their breath during the movement exercises. This creates a "disconnect" that should be remedied immediately. The movement of the arms must represent the movement of the breath-in-time. The arms and the breath move together at the same speed. We consider these intentional body movement exercises as a physical manifestation of the conscious breathing action. During the intentional breathing exercises, the singer breathes-in slowly over the count of four beats and breathes-out with ease over the count of four beats. (See Intentional Movement Exercises, p. 28.)

3. *Circle of Sound* **in-formed vocalization** can produce a natural and organic vocal tone "in-formed" by the breath. An "in-formed" vocal tone is the outcome of a thoughtfully enacted "inspiration." As the teacher guides the students through the conscious breathing and intentional movement sequences, the traditional arpeggio vocalization sequences will extend the singing practice organically from the breathing-moving exercises through actual phonation.

Breathing-in, the students should be taught to invest their concentration and energy in the quality of their in-breath (inhalation) extended outside the body by the slow intentional body movements enacted by the "breath hands." "Breathing-in-moving-in," the students vocalize a simple ascending-descending major triad using the same time and tempo patterns recommended for the conscious breathing and intentional movement exercises (see notation in the In-formed Vocalization Exercises). The in-breath for vocalization is enacted over the same count of four beats. The arpeggio, however, is vocalized over a count of four beats plus four beats (eight beats). Again, the breathing-in hands moving-in to the micro breath circle and the breathing-out hands singing-out to the macro breath circle should *move on the breath* at the same slow tempo. The final tone of the vocalise is a whole note sustained over four full beats.

The in-formed vocalization exercises are repeated in a variety of keys ascending by half steps. The in-breath of each vocalize may be directed by the teacher's cue with numbers (four beat patterns), inspiring words or dramatic images, or different vowel shapes. This method will be discussed later in Chapter 3.

The repeated vocalizations should be directed slowly and thoughtfully by the teacher. The singers should regularly reflect on the quality of their singing experience in terms of how the tone feels in the body and how the tone sounds around them. When the students breathe consciously, move intentionally and vocalize thoughtfully, they can enjoy the feeling of "letting go" of the tonal outcome rather than trying to find some unknown "tone idyll." (See In-formed Vocalization Exercises, p. 34.)

After a systematic practice has been established and the *Circle of Sound* exercises become routine, students are often able to self-diagnose and independently assess the quality of their own singing experience with a high degree of insight and accuracy. Singers know how the voice sounds from the way the tone feels in the body. When the voice feels "right," it is resonant and everybody knows it! When the singer's conscious breathing and intentional movement exercises are concentrated and purposeful, the singer will enjoy the deep awareness that comes from the repeated and systematic practice.

Grounded in the holistic and unified body-mind-spirit practice encouraged by the *Circle of Sound* contemplative approach to vocal development, singing can be a momentous, compelling, and life-changing experience for all students. We invite you to explore, experiment, and enjoy the important health benefits of the *Circle of Sound* breathing, movement, and vocalization practice.

Circle of Sound Voice Education • 25

The Second Foundation

Circle of Sound
Conscious Breathing Exercises

Practice Description:
Speaking in a slow and relaxed tone of voice, the teacher will slowly guide the student's breathing. With the use of a short breathing poem used to guide the in-breath and the out-breath, the teacher learns to pace the tempo of the breathing instruction to accommodate the group. Each student will eventually relax into his or her own breathing tempo. At the beginning of the breathing practice, the breathing is often too fast and too high. As the group practices breathing together over time, a "group synchronicity" will develop, the breath will gradually slow down and deepen. The guide should allow a few seconds of silence between each breathing poem. It is important to keep a relaxed atmosphere.

Practice Exercises:
Following the recommended stretching exercises outlined in Chapter 6 (page 81), the conscious breathing exercises can begin in a sitting or standing position—always in silence. The eyes are usually closed and the body is comfortably positioned. The feet are flat on the ground shoulder-width apart, and the hands are resting, palms down, on the legs or easily at the sides. The body is relaxed, the shoulders are soft, the chest is open and the spine is tall.

The exercises should be guided in a neutral sounding tone of voice. The breathing poems should be spoken slowly, naturally and rhythmically unmeasured. As the students start breathing-in and breathing-out, the guide should maintain a thoughtful and contemplative presence. As the exercise begins, the students will gradually sense a feeling of calm. As the breathing continues the students will begin to concentrate deeply. Eventually the student's calm and concentration leads to deep listening and understanding.

The breathing poems include the following exercises. These texts may be adapted, abridged or used in any way that helps create calm and concentration. Each exercise can be repeated ad lib until the feeling of calm is fully present. The breathing guide uses this text verbatim or an adaptation of this text such as the one given in the *Practice-in-Action* instruction which follows.

Conscious Breathing

Breathing-in.
Breathing-out.
Key words: In. Out.

Breathing-in deeply.
Breathing-out slowly.
Key words: Deep. Slow.

Breathing-in calmly.
Breathing-out with ease.
Key words: Calm. Ease.

Breathing-in smiling.
Breathing-out release.
Key words: Smile. Release.

The Second Foundation

Practice-in-Action (*Guided Instruction*):
Breathing-in, we calm our bodies and ease our minds. We feel our abdomen gently and naturally rising and falling. Breathing-in slowly, our breath deepens and our bodies soften. As we continue to breathe-in and breathe-out, we start to recognize where we are—in the here and in the now. Our worries from the past and our fears of the future fade into a sense of well-being and deep awareness. Breathing-in smiling, breathing-out release, we observe ourselves in the present moment, sitting mindfully. We are peaceful. From our mindful breathing space sitting peacefully, we recognize *where* we are, *what* we're doing, and *who* we're doing it with.

Coaching Notes:
The teacher should participate fully in the breathing exercises. At the same time, it is essential to monitor the students and observe their breathing. The peak of the in-breath is the beginning of the out-breath. The peak of the out-breath is the beginning of the in-breath. Inhalation and exhalation flow continuously and without stopping. At the beginning, some students may stop the breath flow between the in and out breaths. Breathing-in stopping, then breathing-out is incorrect. Be aware of how the breathing eventually slows down and deepens.

The Second Foundation

Circle of Sound
Intentional Movement Exercises

Intentional Movement Practice, Exercise 1
Breathing-In-Breathing-Out-Moving
(Horizontal Space)

Practice Description:
From the benefits of the conscious breathing exercises, the core practice continues seamlessly into the intentional movement forms. As students prepare the body to move on-the-breath, they will stand in a rooted position, centering the body in *wuji* posture.

Wuji Posture

In the *wuji* posture, the feet are firmly grounded, flat on the floor, shoulder-width apart, the head rises like a balloon, the body's center of gravity is lowered as though one were sitting down in a standing position. Enjoying the benefits of continuous breathing in *wuji* posture, raise the arms with the palms of the hands facing in to form a round, ball-shaped circle at the level of the abdomen. In the *Circle of Sound* practice, we call the abdomen the *breath center*, or *dantien*.

Linking the conscious breathing with the intentional movement begins from the position of the arms enacting a large circle space in front of the body at the level of the abdomen. As the student breathes-in, the arms move slowly inward from a large breath circle (macro) to a smaller breath circle (micro). The breathing-in, moving-in, breathing-out, moving-out exercise is sustained slowly over the steady count of four beats in and four beats out. We call these beats *breathing beats*.

The guide will count four beats in and four beats out. The breath circles will move from large breath circle to small breath circle back to large breath circle. This exercise in all three segments creates an immediate and synchronized connection between the movement of the breath and the movement of the body. It is important to note, however, that this process from out-to-in-to-out reverses the traditional understanding of inhalation as expansion and exhalation as contraction. In all phases of *Circle of Sound* there is a constant awareness of open space.

Practice-in-Action (*Guided Instruction*)**:**
Standing in *wuji* posture, rooted and centered, raise your arms with the palms of your hands facing inward to form a large ball-shaped circle in front of your body around your breath center or abdomen. Enjoying the benefits of conscious breathing, soften your knees and lower your body's center of gravity as though you were sitting down while standing. As you shape the large breathing circle in front of you, breathe-in moving your arms slowly inward to form a smaller breath circle in front of you. (The difference in the circle sizes is the difference between a large ball and a smaller ball. Both sizes require open space for air movement.) As you breathe-in slowly, your arms move-in slowly. As you breathe-out slowly, your arms move-out slowly. Our breath circles move from OUT-to-IN-to-OUT. Follow the exercises breathing-in-moving-in over four beats and breathing-out-moving-out over four beats.

Coaching Notes:
This exercise can be guided with the first two conscious breathing poems used (p. 26). We suggest that each of the

The Second Foundation

Intentional Movement Practice, Exercise 1

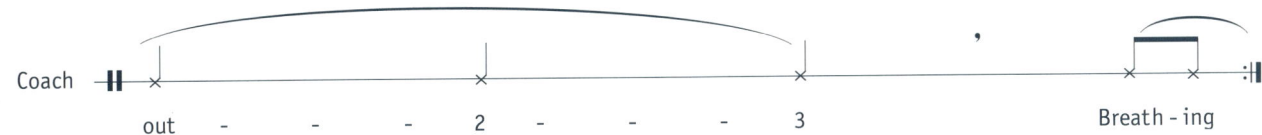

The Second Foundation

breathing-moving exercises be repeated at least six times using two texts: "Breathing-in, breathing-out" (3x) and "Breathing-in deeply, breathing-out slowly" (3x). Using the same conscious breathing texts in guiding the breathing-moving exercises will help the students understand the close relationship between breathing and breathing-moving.

Also, during all the breathing-moving exercises:

1. Observe the students carefully to insure that they do not stop the breath flow at the peak of their in-breath or the peak of their out-breath. Breathing-in and breathing-out should be slow, deep, easy and continuous.

2. Observe the shape of the student's hands and arms to assure that they are "soft" and not tense. Encourage the students to "soften" and curve their arms.

3. Monitor the speed and distance of the arm movement to insure that the movement is the same slow speed as the breath, not faster or slower than the breath. The arm movement is a manifestation of the breath. It is important to develop the synchronicity between speed of the breath flow and the speed of the arm movement.

4. Observe that the moving arms are soft, with the elbow slightly bent.

Intentional Movement Practice, Exercise 2
Breathing-In-Breathing-Out-Moving
(Vertical Space)

Practice Description:
The second intentional movement exercise explores the vertical spaces around us (outside the body) and within us (inside the body). The inspiration for singing derives from multiple sources of energy, including the acoustic and environmental spaces around us, and the biological and physiological characteristics within us. We can conceptualize these energy sources for singing holistically by envisioning them contextually as a circle or medicine wheel that encompasses the four directions of north, south, east, and west.

In singing, the rounded vertical space of the vocal tract can be imagined as the singer consciously breathes-in-and breathes-out-moving. As the breathing-moving exercise is repeated, the student gradually develops an awareness of the open spaces within the vocal tract.

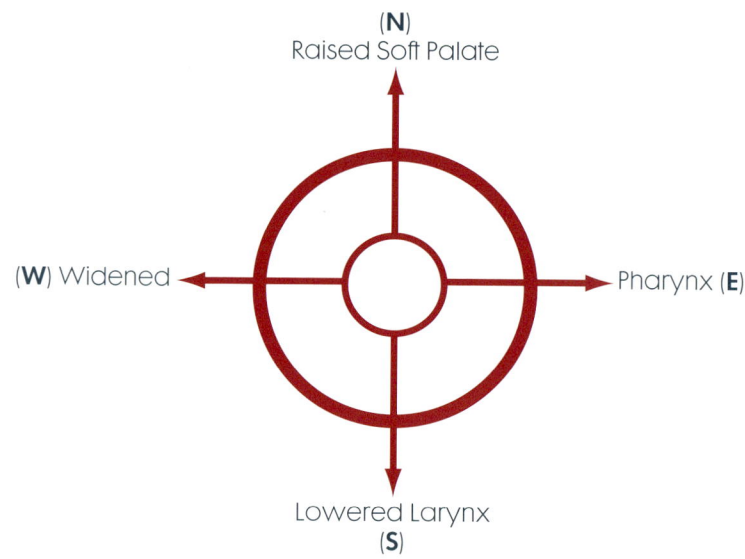

Imagining the vocal tract as the "circle within"

This exercise uses the hand-arm movement in a cylindrical vertical motion from up to down and back up, outlining a vertically shaped circle. This movement is done with what we call a *breath hand* motion starting with the right hand in a softly rounded, arched shape gently positioned next to the face. The *breath hand* moves out, down, around, and back up kinesthetically enacting the often elusive internal processes that cannot be seen or felt by the singer. These gross external motor movements mirror the internally lowered larynx and the raised soft palate during inhalation. The conscious breathing and intentional movement exercise naturally inspires the internal movements of the lowered larynx, and lifted soft palate. As the *breath hand* circles downward, around and back up to the face, the motion of this movement exercise tells the body and mind what the larynx and soft palate are doing inside the open vocal tract during respiration. The arched-

The Second Foundation

Intentional Movement Practice, Exercise 2

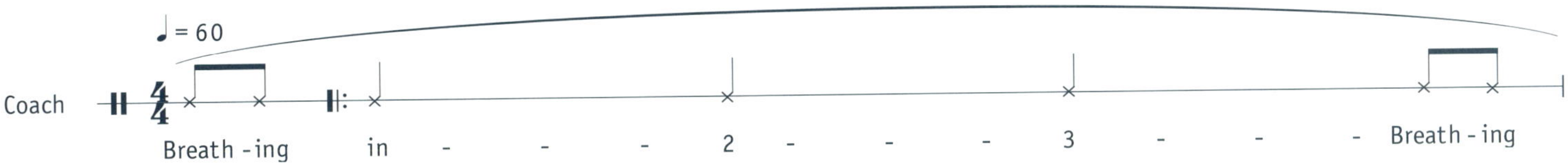

Coach | ♩ = 60 | 4/4 | Breath-ing | in | — | — | — | 2 | — | — | — | 3 | — | — | — | Breath-ing

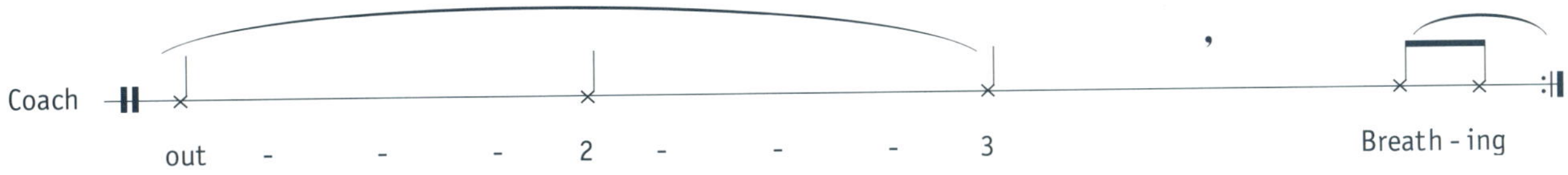

Coach | out | — | — | — | 2 | — | — | — | 3 | | Breath-ing

Circle of Sound Voice Education • 31

The Second Foundation

shape formation of the *breath hand* moving helps the singer imagine the rising soft palate and the forward movement of the tongue.

Practice-in-Action (*Guided Instruction*):
Beginning in *wuji* posture we will explore the vertical space around us and within us. In this exercise you will use the circular hand-arm movement in a rounded vertical motion outlining a vertical space by moving the hand out forward, around downward and back up to the face, parallel to the vocal tract. With your *breath hand* motion your right hand is lifted upwards in a softly rounded, arched shape gently positioned next to the face. Breathing-in, the *breath hand* moves out, (palms out) down, around and back up to the face. Breathing-out, the *breath hand* makes small, micro-circles near the face. Breathing-in, the exercise is repeated.

Coaching Notes:
Practiced in sequence with Intentional Movement Exercise 1, the two breathing-moving formations together create the full circle: Exercise 1 explores the horizontal motion representing the east-west motion of the widened pharynx. Exercise 2 explores the vertical motion representing the north-south motion of the raised soft palate and lowered larynx. All movements are initiated on the breath and defined by the horizontal and vertical motions of the exercises. These intentional movement exercises encourage a growing sense of internal space as the context for singing tone.

Intentional Movement Practice, Exercise 3
Breathing-In-Breathing-Out-Moving
(Horizontal Space-repeated)

Practice Description:
The third breathing-moving exercise brings us back home to the familiar comfort of the first set of exercises. As you shape the large breathing circle in front of you, breathe-in moving your arms slowly inward to form a smaller *breath circle* in front of you. As you breathe-in slowly, your arms move-in slowly. As you breathe-out slowly, your arms move-out slowly. Follow the exercises breathing-in, moving-in over four beats and breathing-out, moving-out over four beats. This exercise can use the text of the conscious breathing poems used earlier, this time changing the text to "breathing-in calm, breathing-out ease" (3x) and "breathing-in-smiling, breathing-out release" (3x).

Practice-in-Action (*Guided Instruction*):
Standing in *wuji* posture, rooted and centered, raise your arms with the palms of your hands facing inward to form a large circle in front of your body around your breath center. Soften your knees and lower your body's center of gravity as though you were sitting down while standing. From the open space of your large breath circle, breathe-in-moving your arms slowly inward to form a smaller *breath circle* in front of you. As you breathe-in slowly, your arms move-in slowly rounded into the smaller breath circle. From the open space of your small breath circle (micro circle), breathe-out slowly moving the arms out slowly back to the large breath circle (macro circle). Follow the exercises breathing-in-moving-in over four beats and breathing-out-moving-out over four beats.

Coaching Notes:
This exercise can be guided with texts from the conscious breathing poems. We suggest that each of the breathing-moving exercises be repeated at least six times using the same two texts: "breathing-in calm, breathing-out ease" (3x), "breathing-in-smiling, breathing-out release" (3x). Using the same conscious breathing texts in guiding the breathing-moving exercises will help the students understand the close relationship between breathing and breathing-moving.

32 • Circle of Sound Voice Education

The Second Foundation

Intentional Movement Practice, Exercise 3: Breathing-In-Breathing-Out-Moving

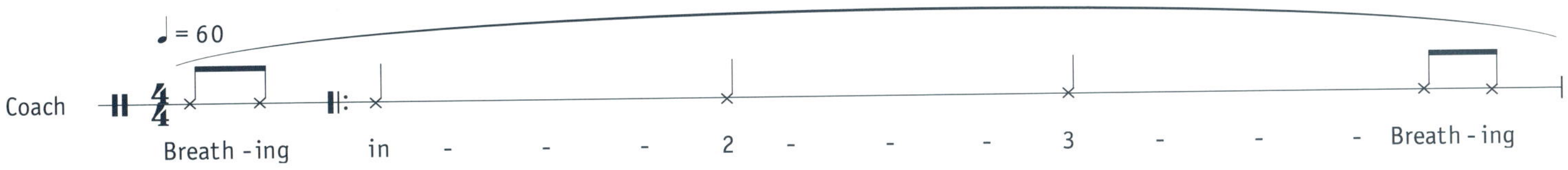

Circle of Sound Voice Education • 33

The Second Foundation

Circle of Sound
In-formed Vocalization Exercises

Practice Descriptions: The conscious breathing and intentional movement exercises, combined with the vocalizations, will motivate and inspire an in-formed vocal tone. Consciously breathing-in, the singers are guided to invest their concentration and energy on the *quality of inhalation*, as demonstrated by the slow intentional movements enacted by the *breath hand's* moving-in and moving-out. Breathing-in-moving-in slowly over four beats, the singers then vocalize the simple patterns moving-out-singing-out over eight beats. The vocalizations are repeated in a variety of keys, cued variously on numbers, words, and vowel shapes. The repeated vocalization exercises are developed to be sung slowly and thoughtfully, giving the singer an opportunity to reflect on the quality of the singing experience. When the singer breathes consciously, moves intentionally, and vocalizes thoughtfully, she can enjoy "letting go" of the tonal outcome. Generally, the singer is able to diagnose and assess her own singing experience with a certain degree of accuracy. She knows from the way the tone feels, whether it's "right." If her breathing and movement exercises are concentrated and purposeful, and if the singer enjoys the deep awareness that comes from repeated practice of conscious breathing and intentional body movement, the vocalization will authentically reflect her entire being.

The informed vocalization exercises are shown interactively for the singer (arpeggio notation), the coach (spoken directions) and the accompanist (piano support). The exercises should proceed in time (ca ♩ = 60) without a break between keys.

Practice-in-Action (*Guided Instruction*): Breathing-in-moving-in, breathing-out-moving-out, we feel the calm concentration of deep breathing and the rooted quiet of slow moving in time and space. Connected from the breath center to the open spaces within us and around us, we are prepared to sing. Breathing-in-moving-in deeply through four-beats, we sing-out-move-out slowly on the pitches *doh-mi-sol* sung on the (ah) vowel over eight-beats. Breathing-in-moving-in on four beats, we move-out-sing-out slowly over eight beats, enjoying the feeling of moving through space and time. Repeating in-formed vocalizations on different pitches using different breathing-in cues (e.g., "breathing-in," "breathing-in-deeply," "breathing-in-smiling") combined with a variety of singing-out cues (e.g., "ah," "oo," "ee") we sense the benefits of a balanced yin-yang relationship in the vocalism. Breathing-in, our inhalation is active and intentional (yang). Singing out, our vocalization is free and easy (yin). When we breathe consciously and move intentionally, the inhalation is more purposeful (yang) and our vocalization is more informed and balanced (yin-yang).

Practice-in-Summary: We hope that you will enjoy the experience of reading and practicing the *Circle of Sound* breathing, movement, and vocalization exercises. We invite you to experiment, explore, and affirm your own artistry and humanity through the *Circle of Sound*. If you listen deeply to your Self, your body will tell you when your singing is "right." The body remembers. Singing that is grounded in a unified body-mind-spirit approach can be a momentous, compelling, and life-changing experience. Your singing is who you are. It is your character and your identity. Singing is a way of enacting your entire being.

The symbol below is used in *Circle of Sound* vocalization to denote "breathing beats." For definition of "breathing beats," see page 22.

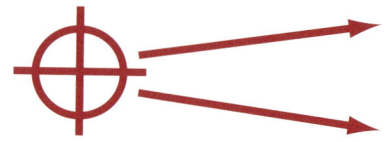

The Second Foundation

Informed Vocalization Practice, Exercise 1 (Arpeggios on Beats)—pg 1

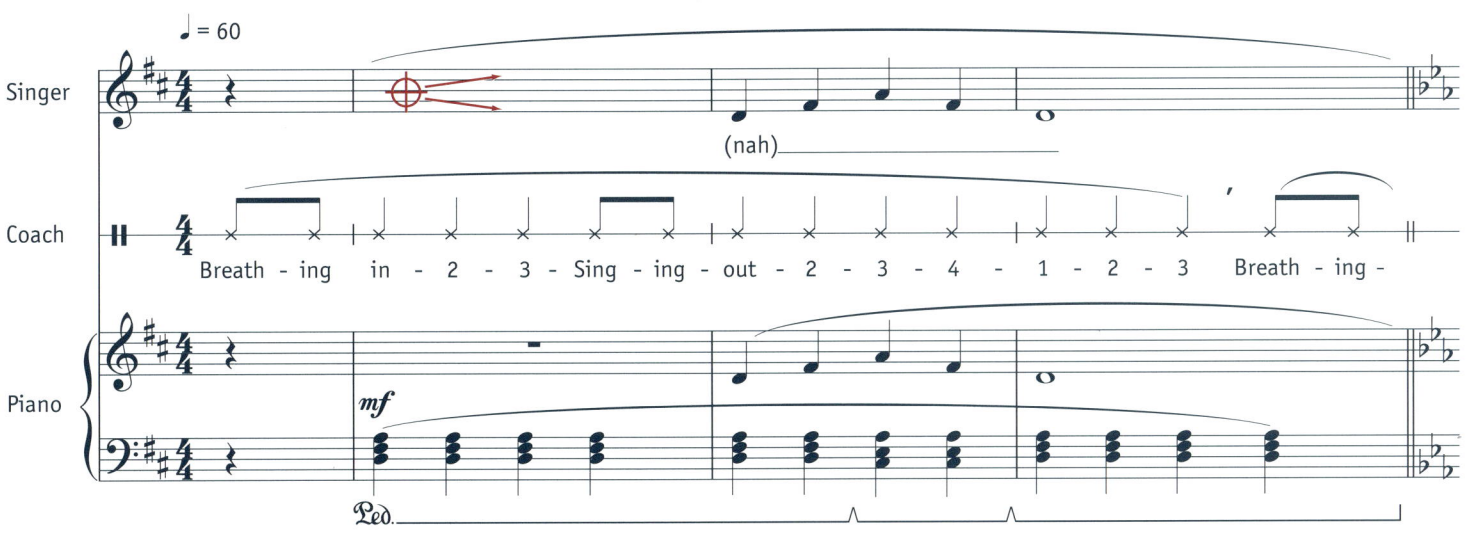

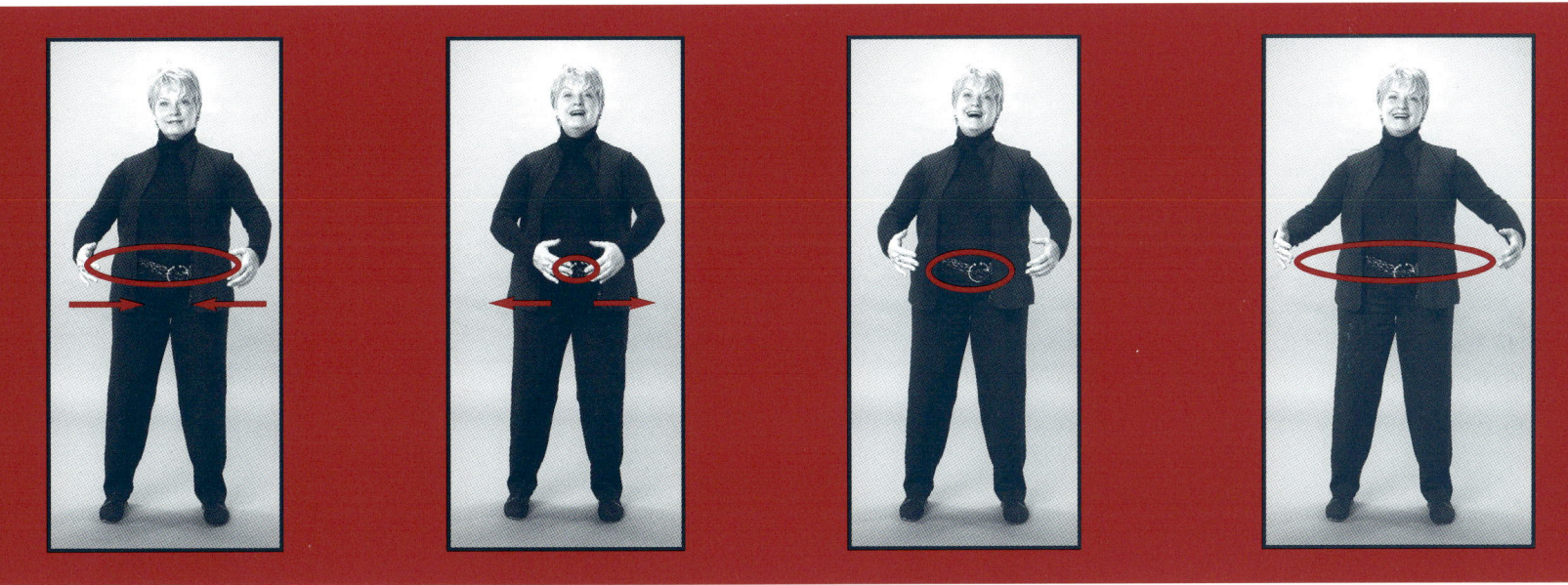

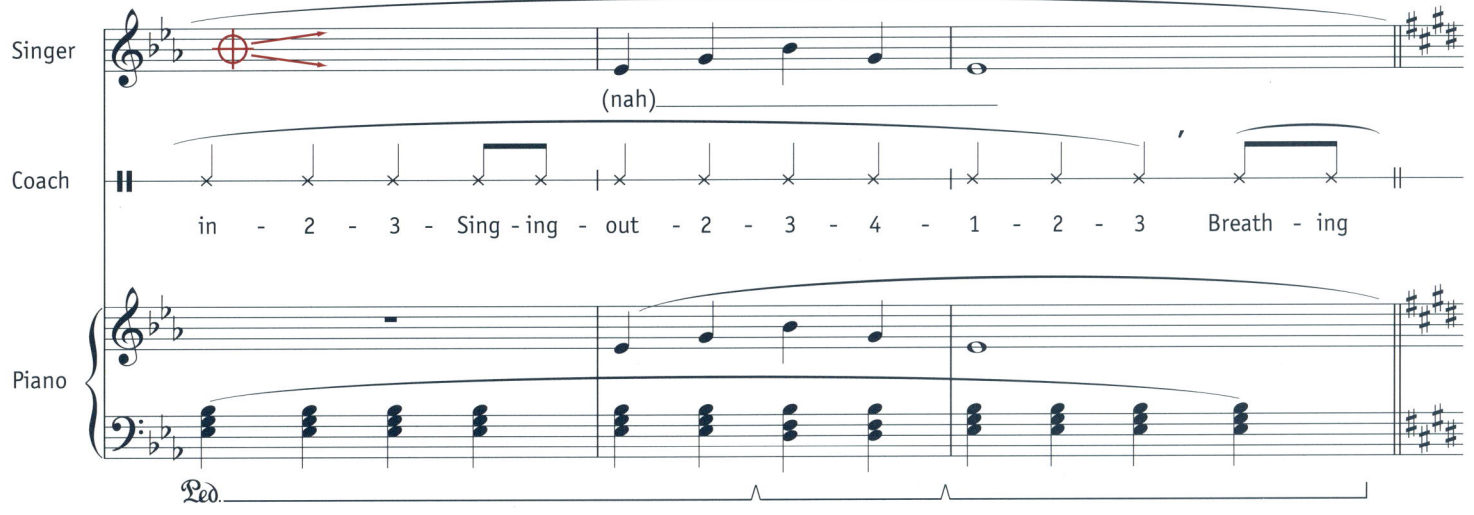

Circle of Sound Voice Education • 35

The Second Foundation

Informed Vocalization Practice, Exercise 1 (Arpeggios on Beats)—pg 2

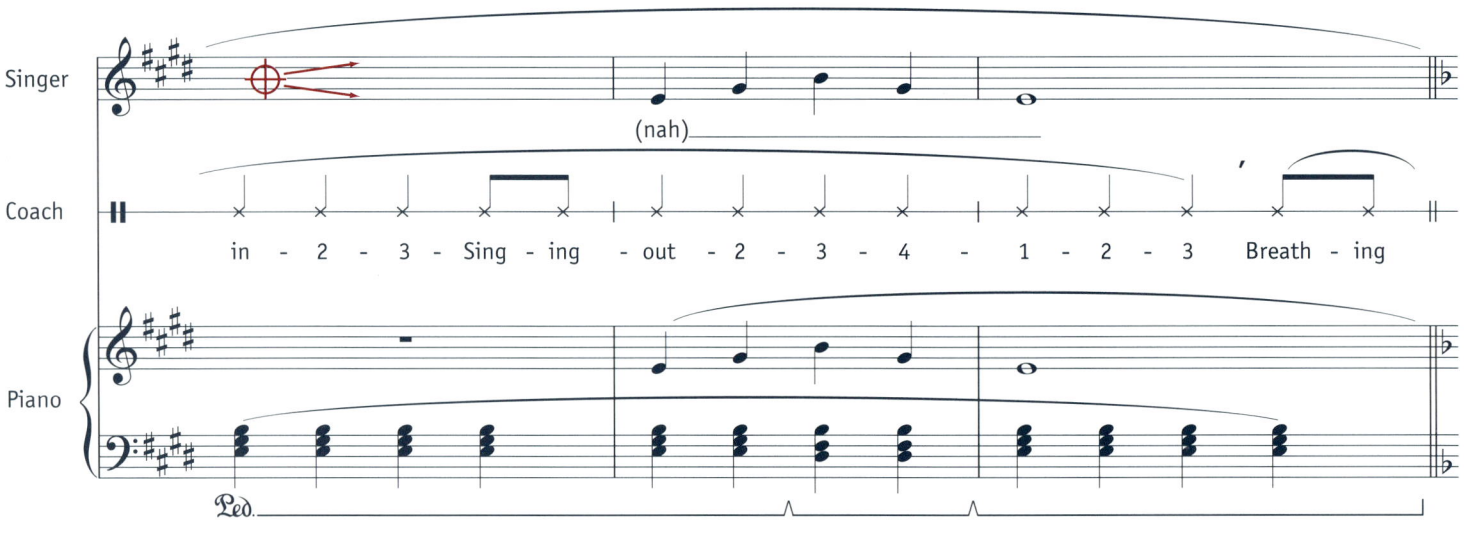

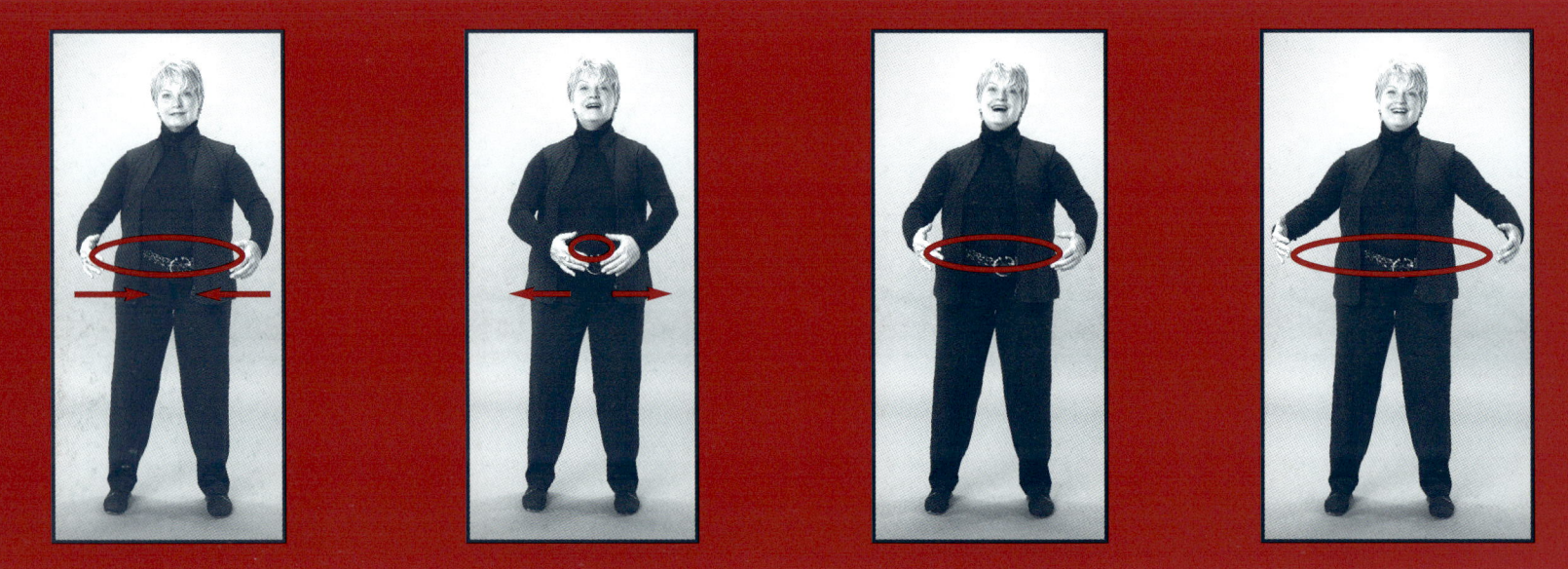

The Second Foundation

Informed Vocalization Practice, Exercise 1 (Arpeggios on Words)—pg 1

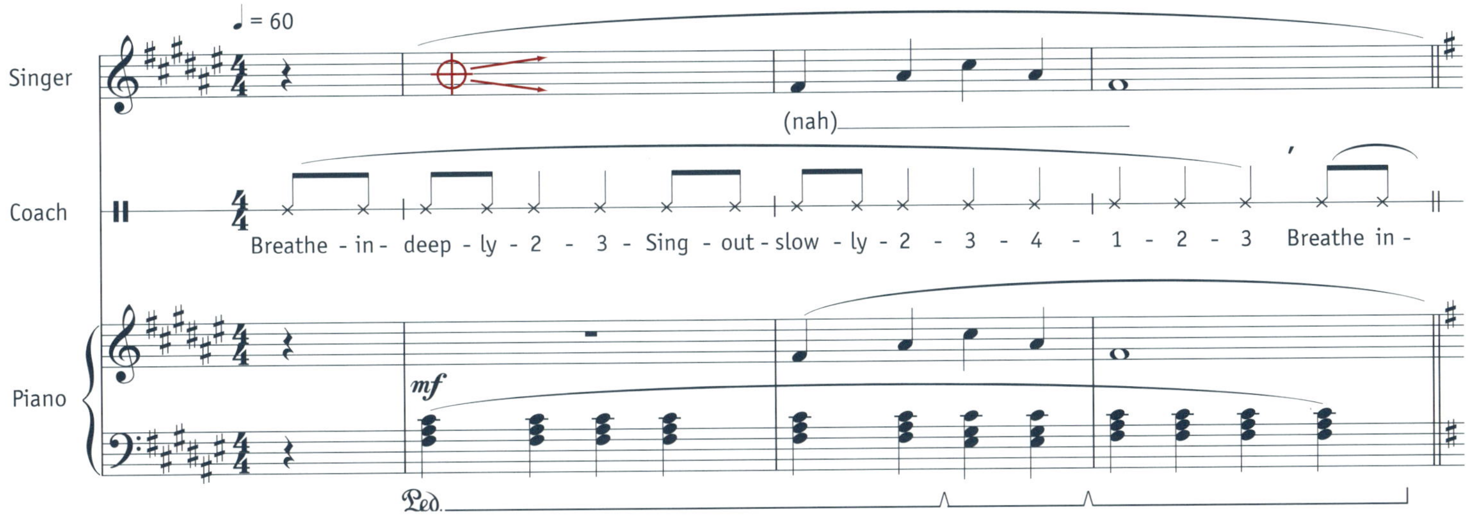

Coach: Breathe - in - deep - ly - 2 - 3 - Sing - out - slow - ly - 2 - 3 - 4 - 1 - 2 - 3 Breathe in -

Coach: calm - 2 - 3 - Sing - out - ease - 2 - 3 - 4 - 1 - 2 - 3 Breathe - in -

Circle of Sound Voice Education • 37

The Second Foundation

Informed Vocalization Exercise 1 (Arpeggios on Words)—pg 2

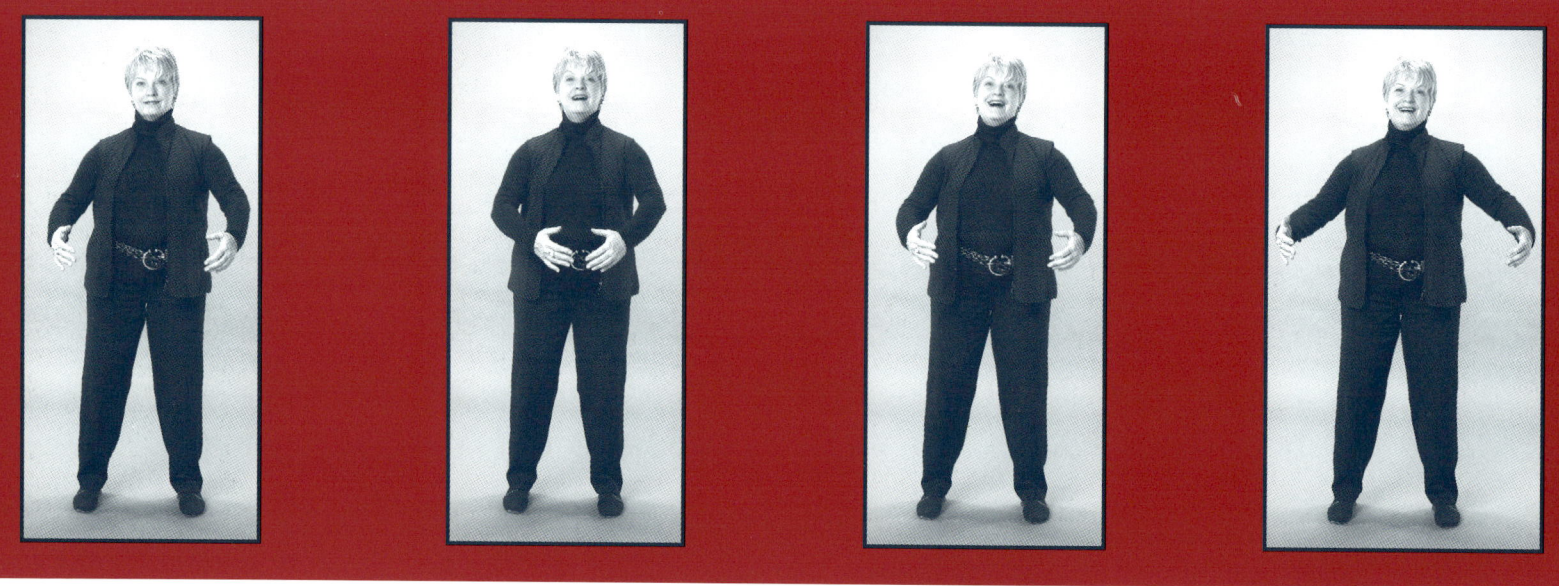

38 • Circle of Sound Voice Education

The Second Foundation

Informed Vocalization Exercise 1 (Arpeggios on Vowels)—pg 1

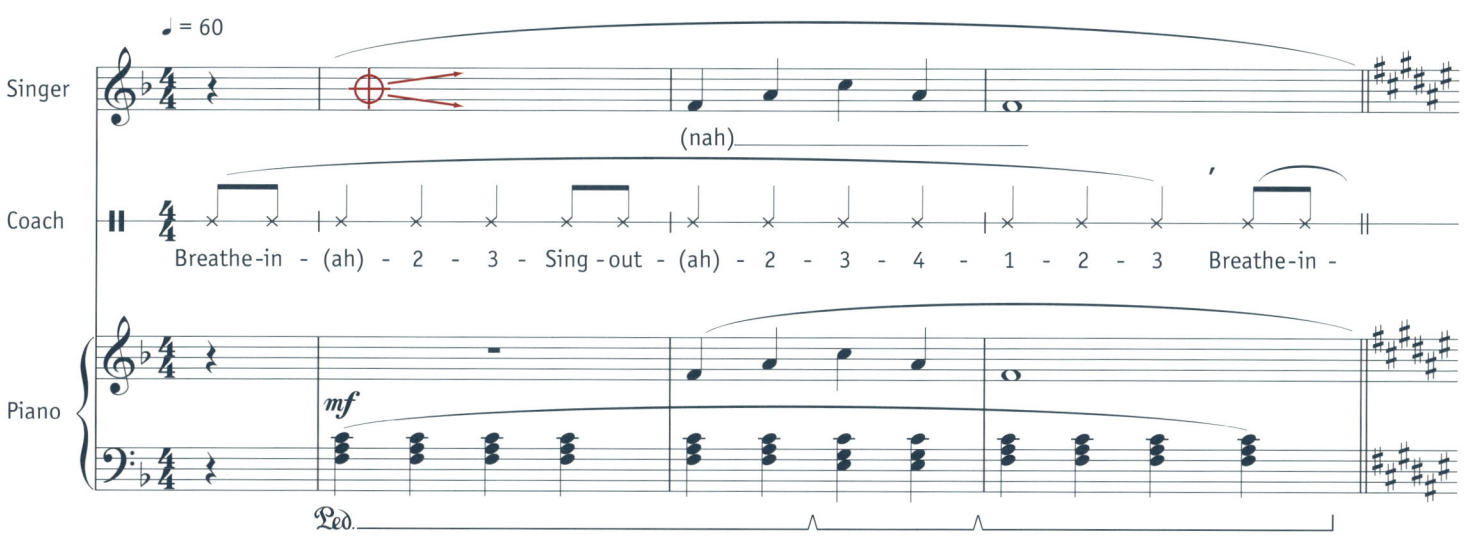

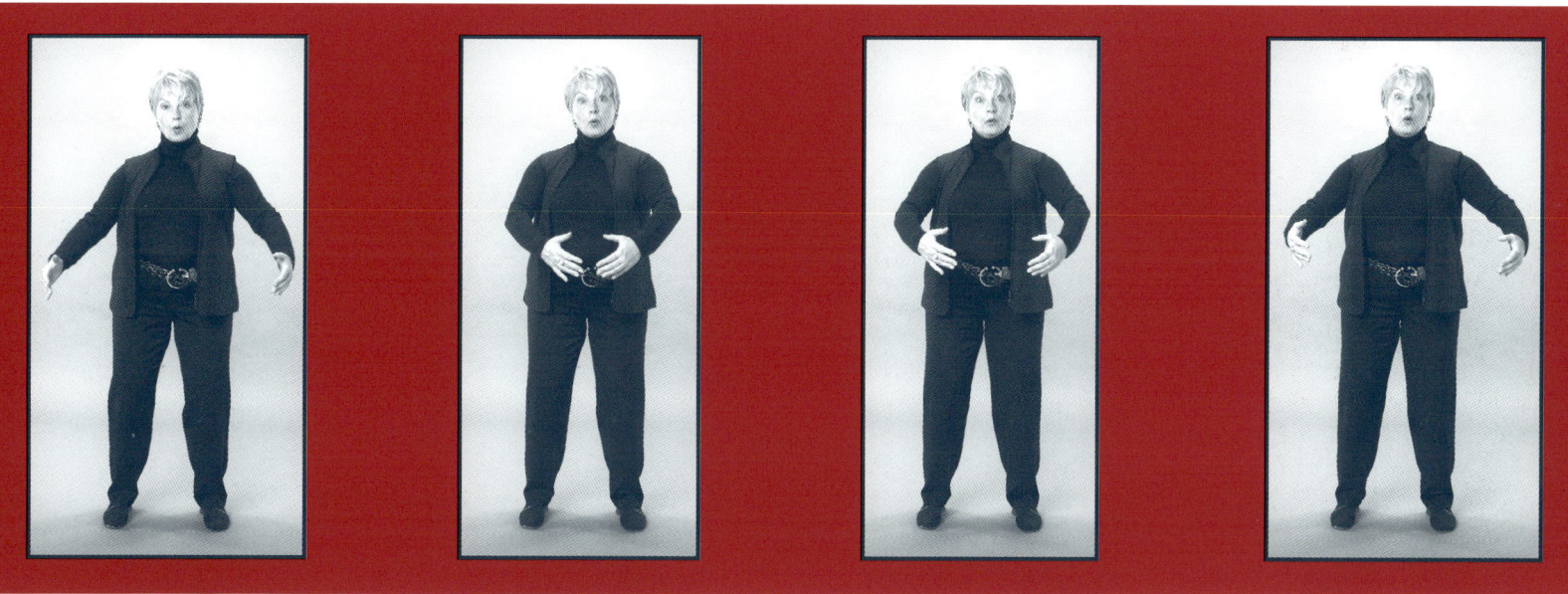

Circle of Sound Voice Education • 39

The Second Foundation

Informed Vocalization Exercise 1 (Arpeggios on Vowels)—pg 2

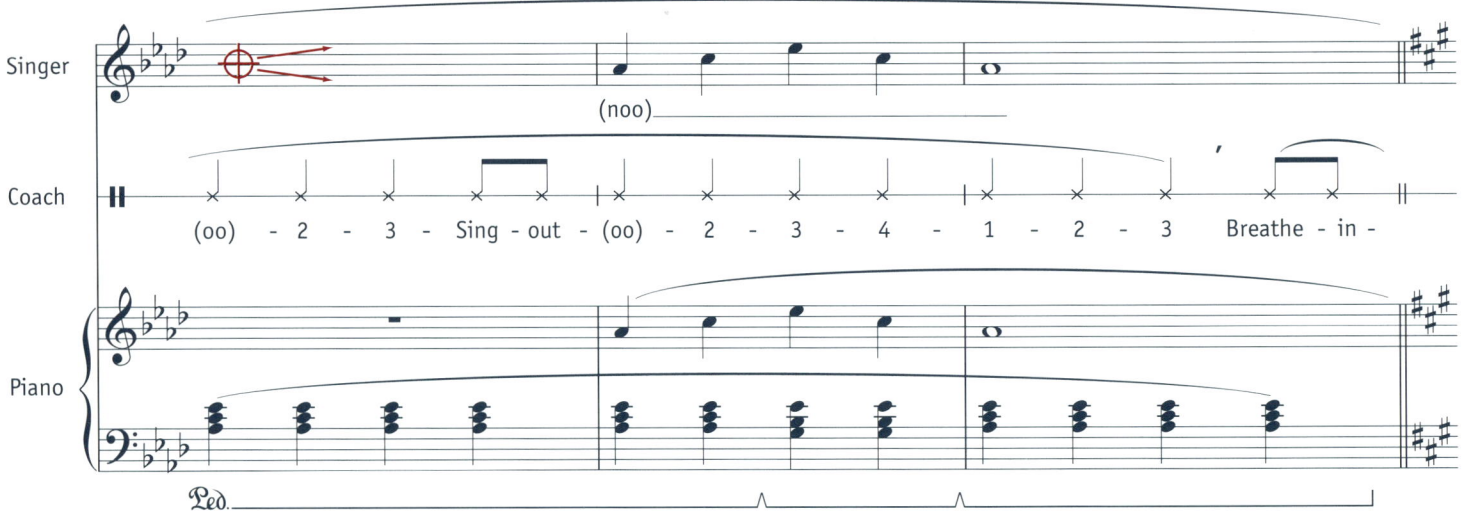

40 • Circle of Sound Voice Education

The Second Foundation

Informed Vocalization Exercise 1 (Arpeggios on Vowels)—pg 3

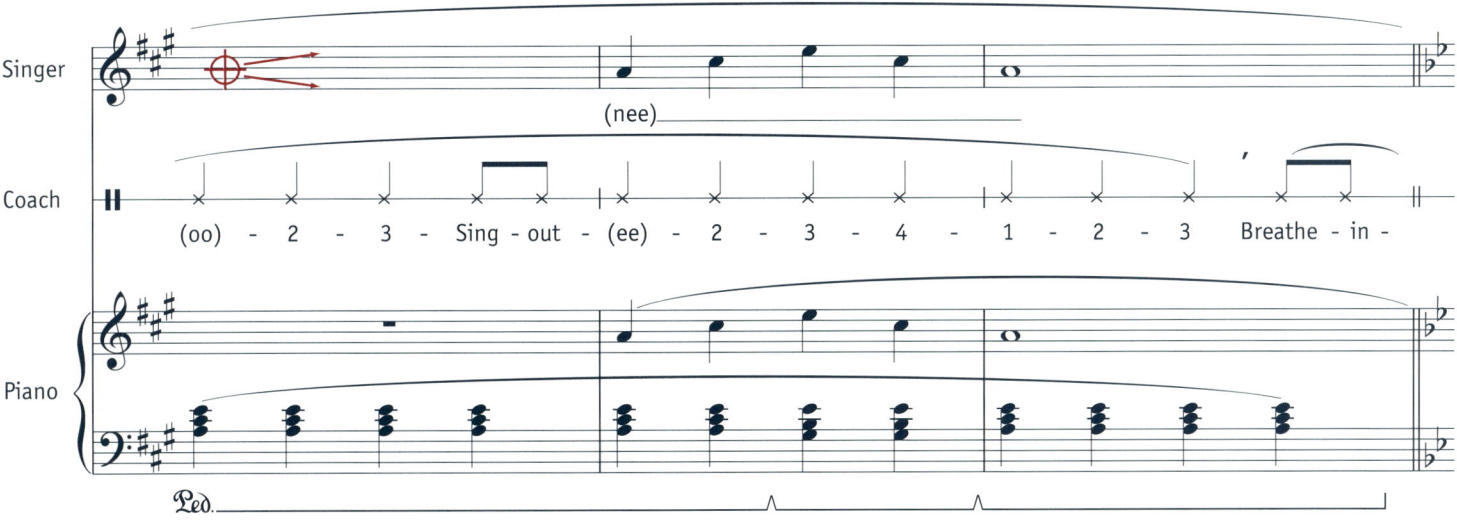

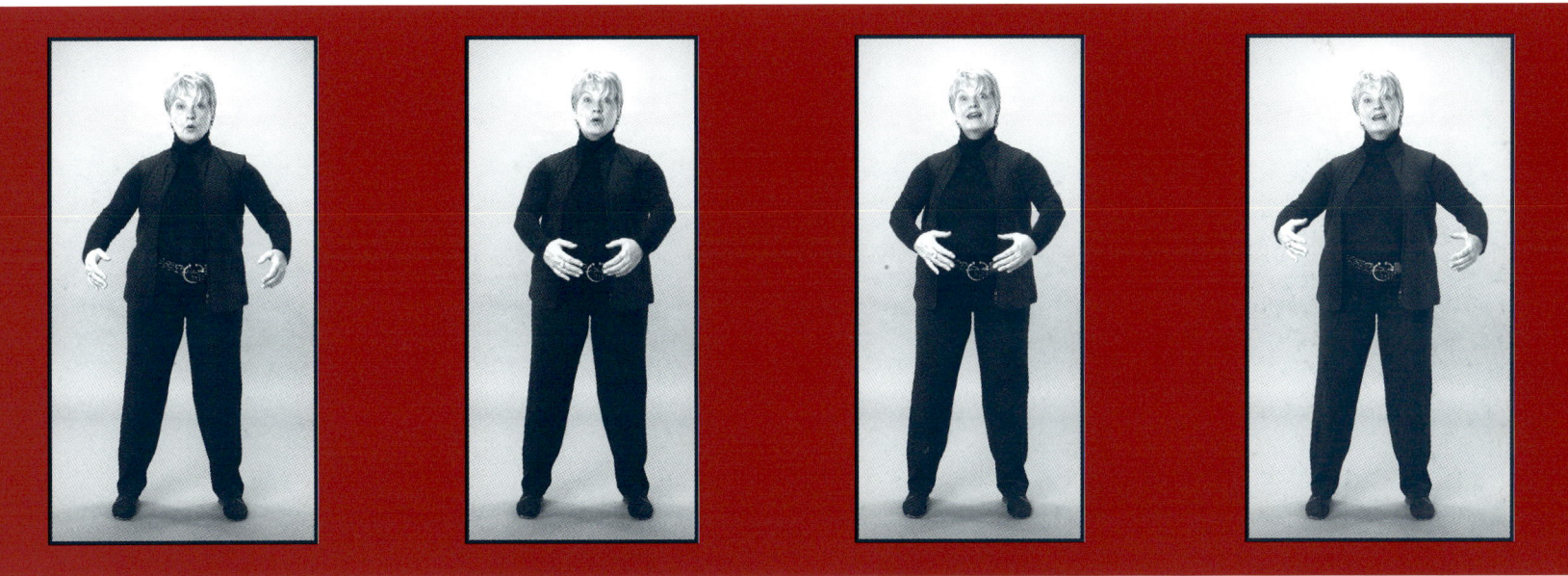

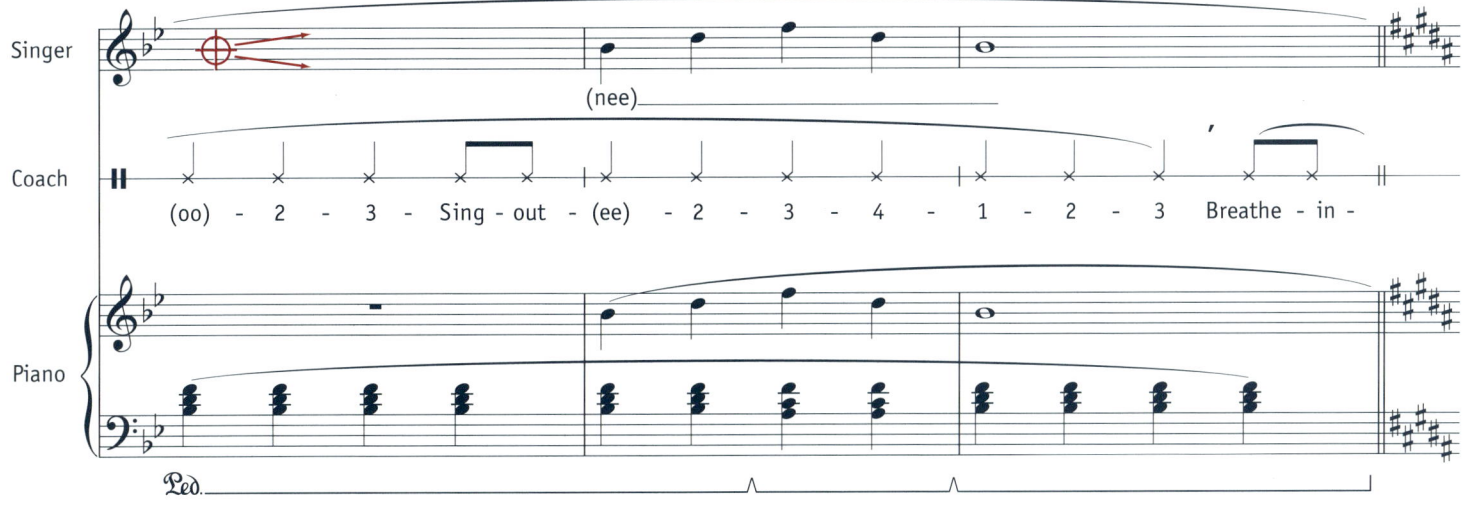

Circle of Sound Voice Education • 41

The Second Foundation

Informed Vocalization Practice, Exercise 1 (Arpeggios on Vowels)—pg 4

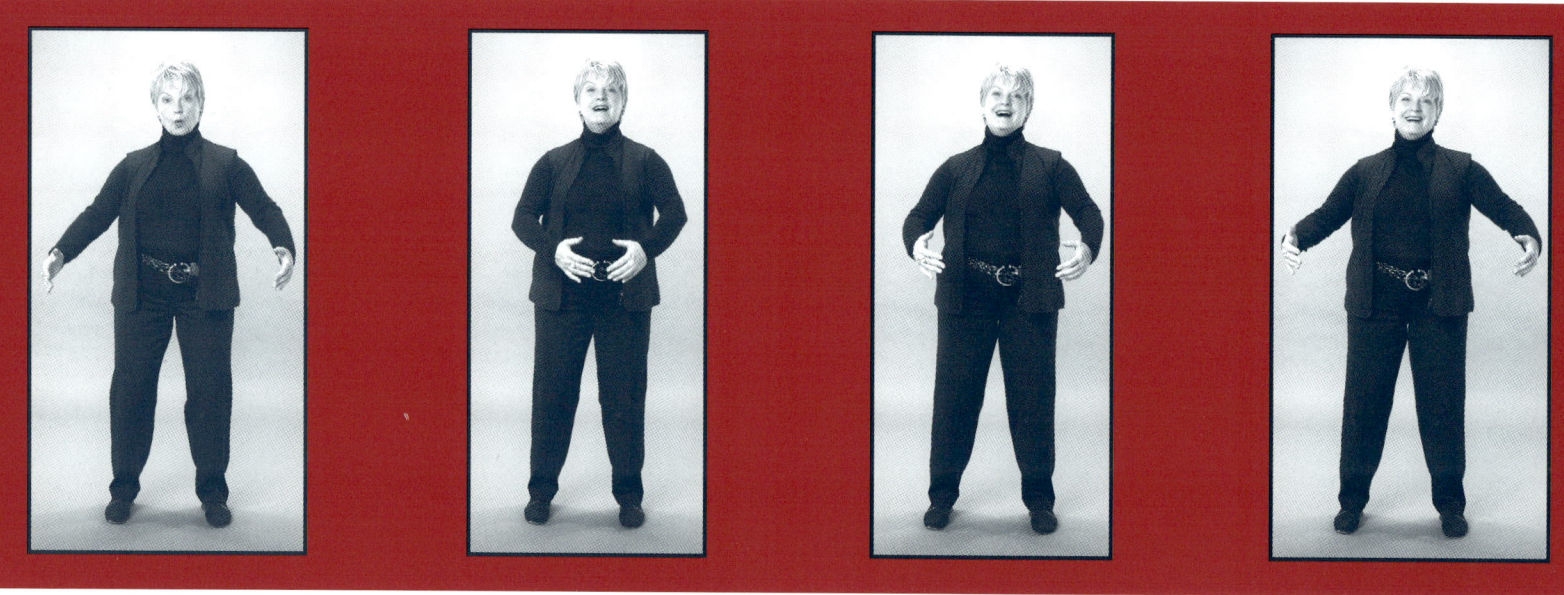

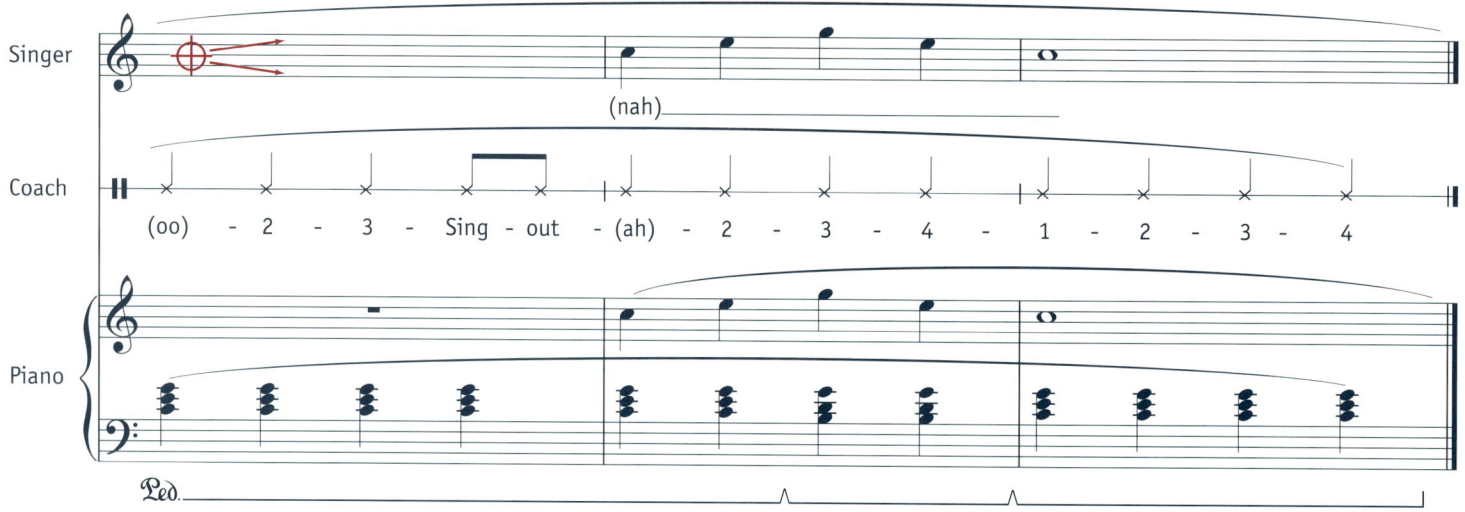

The Second Foundation

Informed Vocalization Practice, Exercise 2 (Five Note Descending Scale)—pg 1

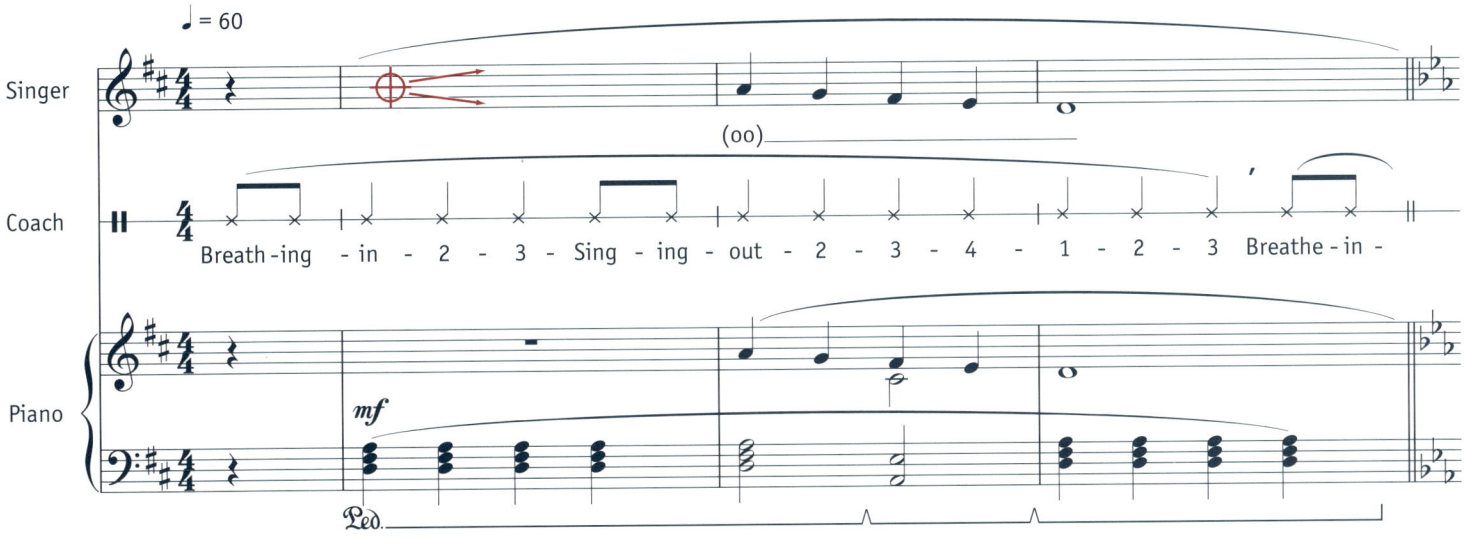

Breath-ing - in - 2 - 3 - Sing-ing - out - 2 - 3 - 4 - 1 - 2 - 3 Breathe-in -

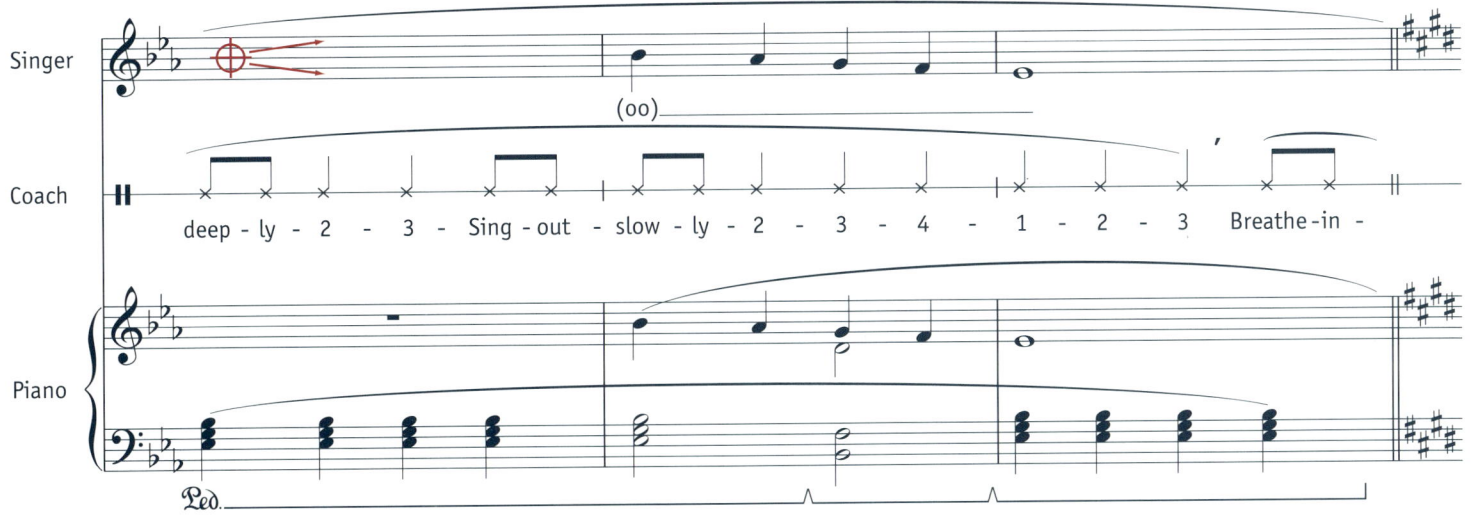

deep-ly - 2 - 3 - Sing-out - slow-ly - 2 - 3 - 4 - 1 - 2 - 3 Breathe-in -

Circle of Sound Voice Education • 43

The Second Foundation

Informed Vocalization Practice, Exercise 2 (Five Note Descending Scale)—pg 2

44 • Circle of Sound Voice Education

The Second Foundation

Informed Vocalization Practice, Exercise 3 (Repeated Unison)—pg 1

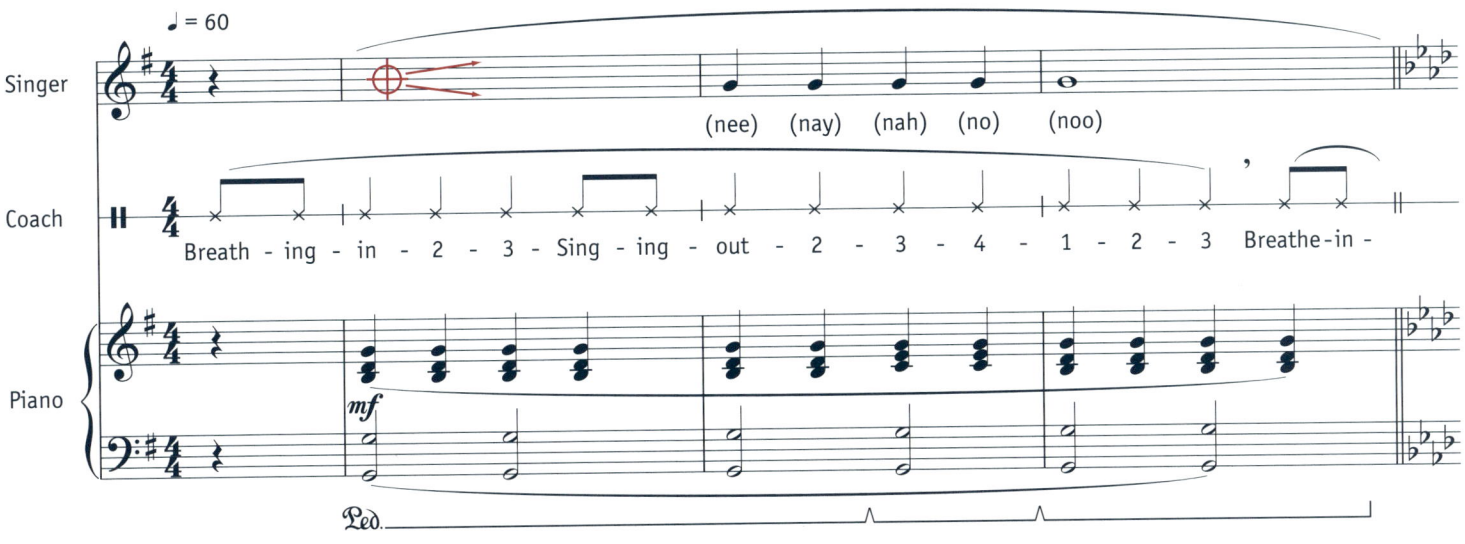

(nee)   (nay)   (nah)   (no)   (noo)

Throughout Exercise 3, arm motion should continue as in Exercise 1.

Circle of Sound Voice Education • 45

The Second Foundation

Informed Vocalization Practice, Exercise 3 (Repeated Unison)—pg 2

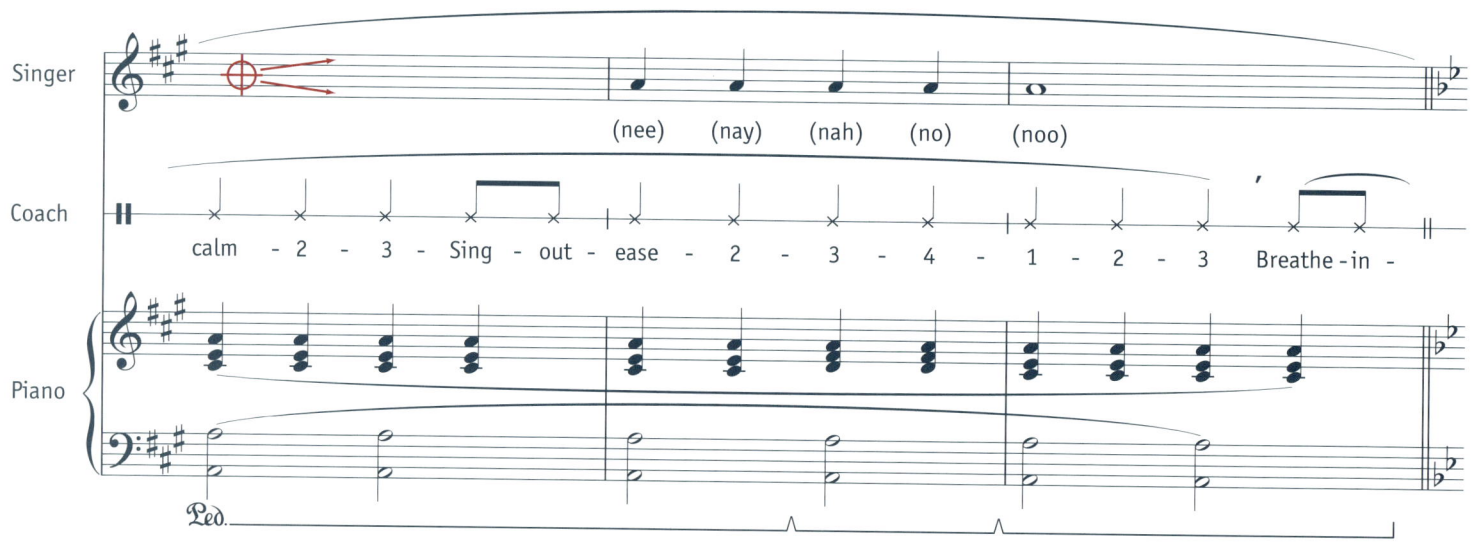

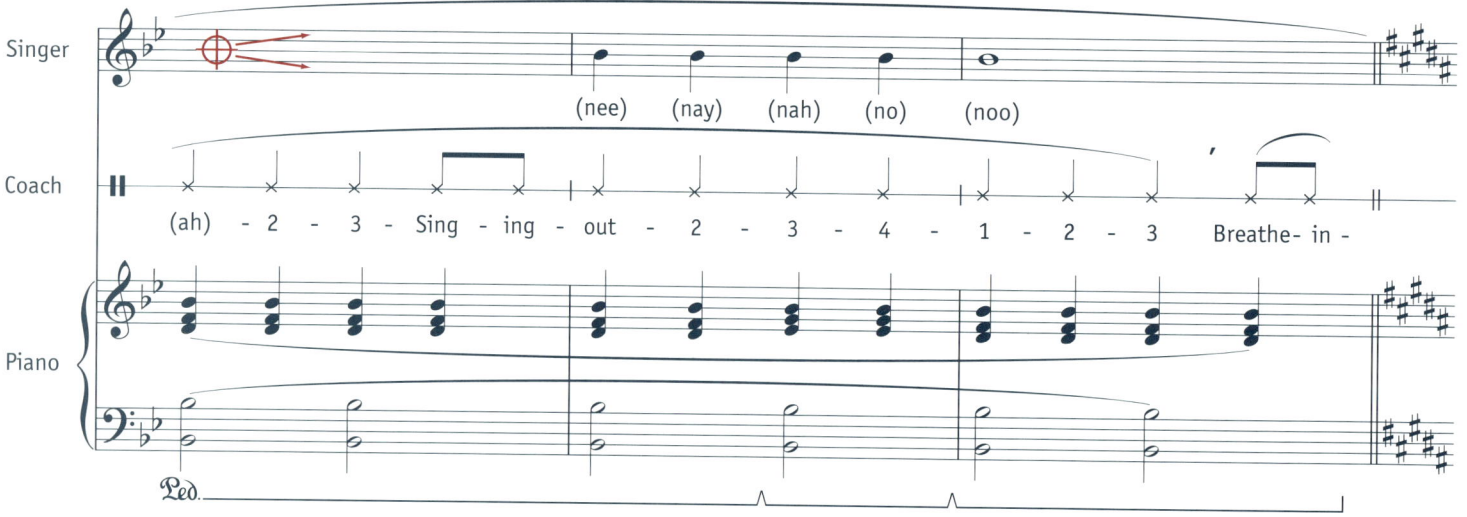

The Second Foundation

Informed Vocalization Practice, Exercise 3 (Repeated Unison)—pg 3

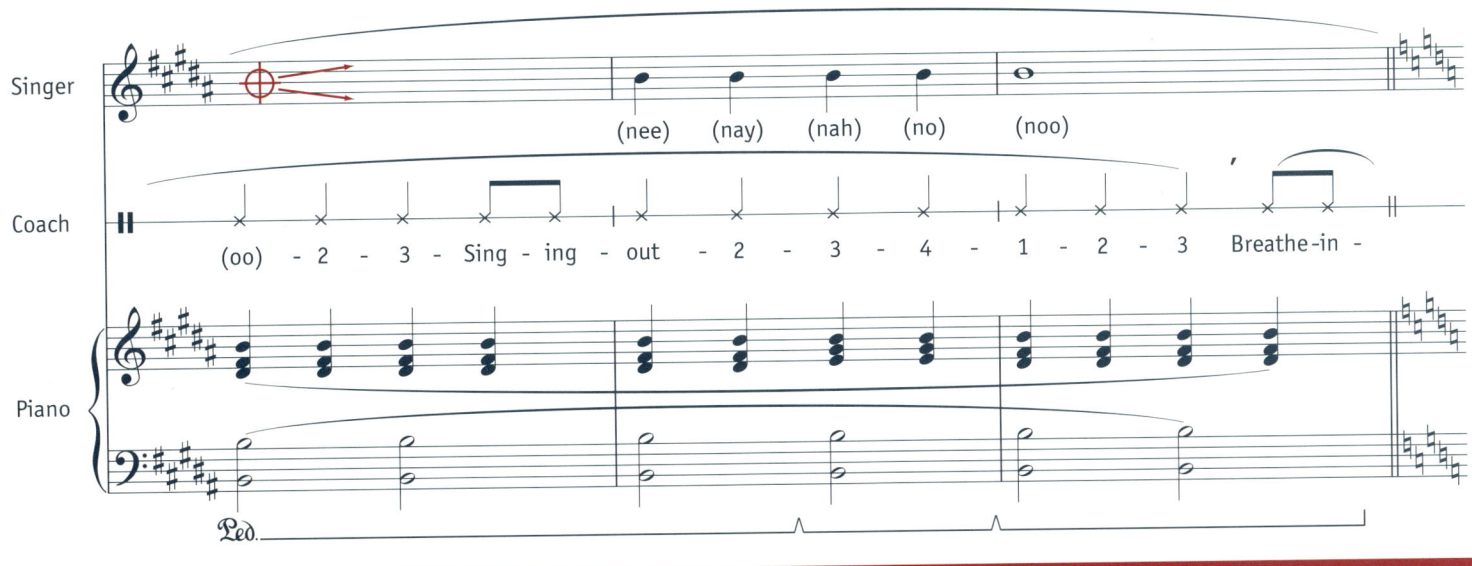

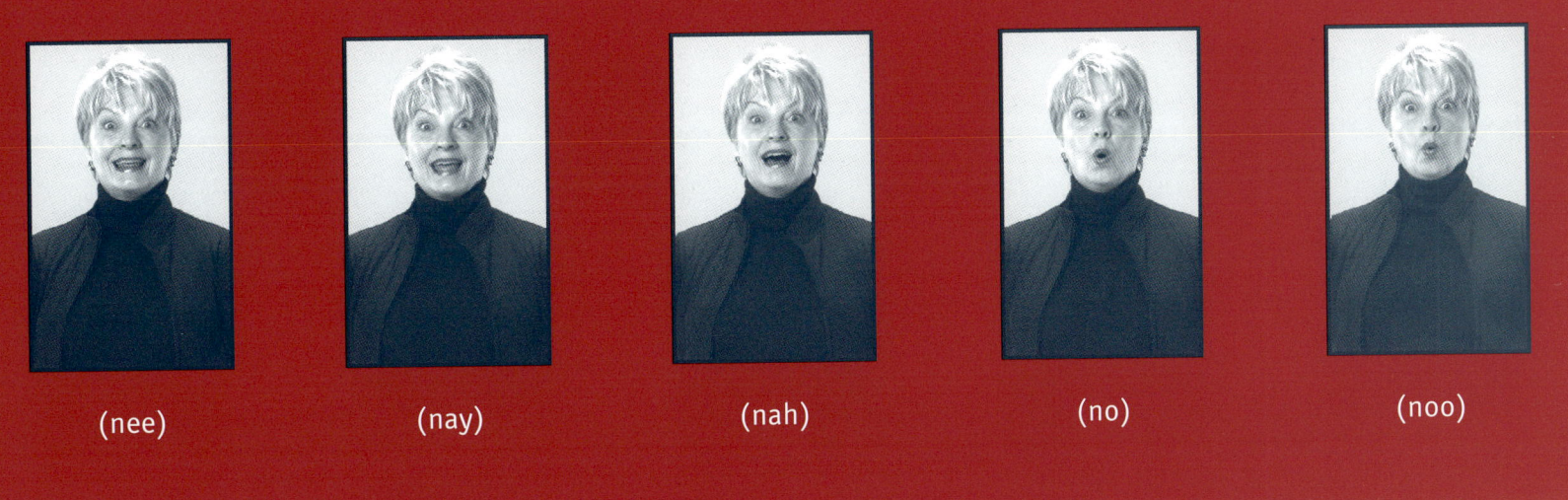

(nee) (nay) (nah) (no) (noo)

Chapter 4
The Third Foundation: Deep Listening
Circle of Sound Extended Practice (In Rehearsal and Performance)

Circle of Sound Voice Education is more than a series of breathing and movement exercises designed to calm the body and release the voice for singing. As a contemplative approach to singing, *Circle of Sound* considers the quality of the singer's musical experience, not just in education, but in life.

With the evolution of the new millennium, there is no escaping the catastrophes and suffering that surround us at home and abroad. In this United Nations Decade for the Culture of Peace and Non-violence, it is time to explore the role of singing in the musical experience of our youth beyond the limitations of prescribed educational constructs or popular methodological trends. These often disembodied approaches were generated in a past unconnected to the environmental, social or political realities of our time. Too many of us have performed and taught for too long in isolation from the enormous suffering, violence, and depression that exists around us.

Scholars in the field of emotional intelligence tell us that the present generation of children are more troubled emotionally, more lonely and depressed, more angry and prone to worry than at any time in history.[1] In light of these realities, how then should we consider singing and the musical experience of our children and youth in *the here and the now*—in education, in life and *for* life?

We've talked about awareness and the importance of the student's ability to observe her own thought processes, her emotions and her internal states through conscious breathing meditation or mindfulness practice. Listening, like awareness, is closely related to the singer's ability to pay attention, to calm the body and the mind, to recognize feelings and to attend to the singing processes without fear and anxiety. Deep listening is closely related to awareness. Once the singer "comes home" to the breath, she is able to listen deeply to herself and to others.

In the *Circle of Sound* core practice (Chapter 3), we introduced a *Circle* vocabulary based on the lived musical experience of singing. The authors purposely avoided using traditional terminology in an effort to avoid possible tensions that may be associated with prescriptive pedagogies from the past. By avoiding technical language, and by using a vocabulary derived from lived musical experience, we believe we have a better chance of helping students avoid the fear and anxiety often associated with the performance experience.

In preparation for the application of *Circle of Sound* to rehearsal and performance settings, we will begin with a review of the four foundations of this approach framed in the context of a short essay on singing. This summary and review will be followed with a sampling of rehearsal and performance techniques using selected musical excerpts.

The Third Foundation

Circle of Sound in Review: Beyond Thinking

Circle of Sound is based on a dynamic model of singing as a form of personal *awareness*, as an act of *mindfulness*, as an exercise of *deep listening*, and as the experience of *well-being*. This is not to say that the traditional values of singing as *musicianship*, as the practice of *skill and understanding*, and as a *form of knowledge* or *thinking-in-action* are absent from a contemplative approach to singing. We are suggesting, however, that *Circle of Sound Voice Education* is a multidimensional view of singing that goes beyond thinking, beyond the command of vocal technique, and beyond the learning of notation to include the *singer's ability to recognize his shared humanity with the world*.

Voice education in the world today must necessarily consider the kind of personal attention, emotional support and caregiving that motivates our student's ethical discernment—their ability to embrace a moral course of action. It is more important than ever that we consider singing as a matter of character and service. If we believe that what we are doing as artists, educators, and teachers is distinctly ethical in character, then our teaching ought to be concerned with the education of our student's personal character and social identity. As writer David Best persuasively argues, education in the arts has an utterly inescapable moral dimension (cited by Wayne Bowman).[2]

What does the development of personal intelligence, ethical discernment, and moral responsibility have to do with *Circle of Sound Voice Education*? In our view, just about everything! *Circle of Sound* addresses singing as a form of awareness, clearly a skill related to personal intelligence. Through the practice of breathing meditation, a simple and systematic series of breathing exercises that encourage the singer to follow his breath in and out for a period of three to eight minutes, the student's awareness of himself and others continually deepens.

Circle of Sound addresses singing as an act of mindfulness—the skillful means of being fully present in the here and the now. Mindfulness and ethical discernment are interdependent skills. Through the sequenced series of breathing, movement, and vocalization exercises, the students learn to bear witness to themselves and to others in their community. They learn to connect with themselves as a way of connecting with others. They learn to slow down, to recognize where they are, to concentrate and to understand the meaning of what it is they are doing.

Circle of Sound teaches the skills of *deep listening* as a form of moral responsibility. As the students practice conscious breathing, they begin to hear the quiet, feel the calm and sense the release of tension and anxiety in their bodies and minds. The ability of the student to listen to others, to the ensemble, to hear their own parts in relation to other parts and to make adjustments in pitch, tone quality, or dynamic levels requires the ability to listen deeply. The ability to listen deeply is closely related to being free of fear and anxiety, being at ease, and being in calm and concentration. These are all qualities that will improve through the systematic practice of *conscious breathing*, *intentional movement*, and *in-formed vocalization*. Learning to listen to the self is the first step in learning to listen to others.

Circle of Sound is the practice of *well-being*. In a world where violence and injustice surrounds us, it is not enough for our students to simply produce beautiful singing for its own sake. Too often our work takes place in the exclusive confines of our rehearsal rooms and concert halls that leave out most of the world. Yes, beautiful singing and the student's ability to produce and respond feelingly to beauty are essential in education and in life. But singing beautiful tones for their own sake is not enough to educate our students' social consciousness or sense of moral responsibility in the world today. Well-being comes from the quality of our connection with others—from the sense of shared humanness that comes from singing together for the benefit of all beings.

The Third Foundation

Therefore, it is without hesitation that we recommend this contemplative approach to voice education as the inclusive education of personal intelligence, ethical discernment, and moral responsibility. Through the practice of *awareness*, *mindfulness*, and *deep listening*, a young singer who recognizes herself as an important part of the world, who is at peace with her surroundings, who respects the multiple differences and the rights of all people to justice and freedom and who demonstrates her service to the community through the joy and pleasure of singing counts in every way as an artist and a peacemaker.

Singing as Listening

Beginning with the concept of singing as a form of deep listening, the *Circle of Sound* breathing exercises prepare the singer physically and emotionally for the experience of singing. When we breathe-in deeply, we empty our minds—we think less and listen more. The past is already gone and the future has not yet arrived. When we breathe-in deeply we are fully present in the here and the now. In the quiet of "not-thinking" we recognize ourselves in the present moment, peaceful and happy. In that moment we begin to relax our bodies and calm our minds. As we calm our minds we are able to listen deeply and "bear witness" to instruction without fear and anxiety.

In both the rehearsal and the studio, singing-as-listening allows the student and teacher to be truly present in musical relationship. For the teacher, listening means being able to receive whatever the student is singing—even the wrong notes sung at the wrong times. Bearing witness to imperfect tone or faulty intonation (or what I call "smiling at the wrong notes") is the first step toward building a relationship of trust, awareness and acceptance. It is also the first step toward building beautiful tone and excellent intonation.

How can a singing student understand how a beautiful tone sounds unless she is able to compare and contrast her "beautiful" tone with her "not-so-beautiful" tone? How can a choir sing in tune without the opportunity to recognize out-of-tune singing and compare it with in-tune singing? When a teacher practices deep listening, she can recognize the "unlearned" and the "imperfect" as the first step in guiding the student toward an awareness of beautiful tone.

As we introduce students to singing-as-listening, we can remind them that musical experience is more than a form of musical thinking or musical doing. Musical experience is a way of *being* musical, and *being* is a psycho-spiritual matter inclusive of mind, body, and spirit. Theories and teaching practices that neglect the bodily and spiritual dimensions of singing in favor of an exclusively cognitive or technical perspective fail to recognize the organic and multidimensional nature of singing as a way of listening musically.

A contemplative approach to singing is concerned with the psycho-spiritual development of the student as an integral part of the singer's voice education. A contemplative singing practice that includes *conscious breathing* and *intentional movement in-forms* the singer's voice and supports her ability to listen. It is in the singer's ability to resource her body's intuitive knowledge and develop trust and confidence in that fundamental connection to herself and the world that she serves humanity—in the studio, in the rehearsal room and in the concert hall—in all of life!

The singer's "relaxed mind," her ability to be fully present in the here and the now, and to listen deeply, connects her to the music she interprets. The singer that practices conscious breathing and intentional movement in a committed and systematic manner is the singer that transcends her fears of inadequacy in favor of singing more beautifully and more devotedly than ever before.

Singing as Relationship-Making

I like to think of singing as a way of life and I would like to think that we can teach singing the way we aspire to live. This seems logical and direct. In life we engage in relationships with our families and friends. Our lives are about relationships and relationship-making. Living beings are culturally situated

The Third Foundation

and we live in communities where we connect in acts of exploration, affirmation, and celebration. Singing as community, as connection, as relationship and relationship-making is the essence of voice education. Singing as relationship-making is the real-life element that forms the root of the vocal arts.

Singing is cultural. It is an inextricably social act. Based on the scholarship of Christopher Small, whose work explores the meaning of musical performance[3] as the ability to bring into existence a set of relationships between the sounds and between the participants, we begin to view singing as a reflection of relationships and relationship-making opportunities. As the singer vocalizes and explores the possibility of her voice, she learns from the sounds she makes as well as the sounds she doesn't make. In affirming those sounds, she goes about developing relationships with the music, with fellow performers, and with her audience.

In *Circle of Sound Voice Education*, we think of singing as a form of relationship-making, inclusive of connecting with ourselves, with others, with the environment and with the world around us. Singing as relationship is a dynamic and vibrant thesis that invites careful consideration.

Singing as Peacemaking

What is peacemaking and how can we teach singing as a form of peacemaking? Peace is more than the absence of conflict. Peace is the presence of connection. Singers must first develop inner peace. Inner peace is about the connection with our true and natural *voice*—our true and natural *selves*. As singers develop inner peace though conscious breathing and mindfulness meditation, they will begin to be at peace with themselves, with the technical demands of the music, and with their audiences.

Singing as peacemaking is a state of mind and a path of action. It is about the quality of relationship that we described earlier; it is personal and musical. As a state of mind, the singer must be *fully present* in the here and the now—present with herself (awareness) and present with others (mindfulness). Through the *Circle of Sound* practice she will learn to *listen deeply* to the music, to the teaching, and to those for whom she sings. She will learn to *embrace the diversity* of vocal tones and musical styles she undertakes as a way of honoring the many different qualities she can achieve vocally and as a way of honoring the diversity of the musical repertoire she performs.

The singer as peacemaker is one who *serves the community* by sharing his voice and his music as a source of joy and pleasure for others and especially for those in need. This singer empowers his audiences by the way he commands the music, affirms the composer's intentions and celebrates the performance occasion with others. This singer is *fully present* and in the world today. In crisis, he sings more beautifully and more devotedly than ever before. This singer finds the cup of ecstasy in places of darkness. This singer is peaceful and happy.

Singing and Transformative Experience

In the *Circle of Sound* contemplative approach to singing there is an integral relationship between the "right" notes and the "wrong" notes. In accepting the limitations of the student's tone or the choir's intonation in the moment, we create an environment of trust, the possibility for self-understanding and the potential for transformative experience—the kind of experience that is generated from the singer's self-knowledge, and not the teacher's demands or prescriptions.

Transformative experience is the highest calling of any educational endeavor. Transformative experience requires that the student's understanding be developed over a period of time, from the "inside-out" versus the "quick fix," prescriptive approach of technically driven pedagogy. To guide the student to become her own teacher, using her own deep listening and inner resources to accept apparent limitations, or create desired change, is an act of deep *caring*. Singing and teaching singing as a form of listening or "bearing witness" is a way of *caring* and being *cared for*. Personal attributes like tolerance, compassion, patience, and the ability to listen closely and

The Third Foundation

empathetically to the student's efforts, are the building blocks of a musical relationship free of fear and anxiety. Transformative experience in singing is available only when there is an environment of non-fear. As Aristotle observed, this approach is "not for every person, nor is it easy."[4]

Circle of Sound Extended Practice In Musical Context

What follows next is the use of conscious breathing, intentional movement, and in-formed vocalization as the *Circle of Sound* core practice continues into the musical context of rehearsal and performance. We describe this continuation as the *Circle of Sound* "extended practice."

In the *Circle of Sound* contemplative approach to singing, the singer learns to "come home" to the breath during the context of the warm-up period. This is what we call the core practice (Chapter 3). As the singer's concentration improves and the mind relaxes, she will start to "come home" to the breath during the context of rehearsing and performing. Eventually, through practice, every moment will be a conscious moment. The singer's voice and the singer's spirit are one.

In rehearsal we adapt the core practice to facilitate healthy vocalism and improve the quality of musical experience. Before we suggest practice applications for rehearsal, we will first review the basic *Circle* vocabulary. *Circle of Sound* practice is inclusive of breathing, movement, and vocalization. While it requires extra effort to think holistically about breathing, movement, and vocalization as one practice, the benefits of this interdependence can be felt and heard in the singing voice almost immediately.

At the conclusion of this section, I will illustrate how various exercises can be used in the context of three selected works: Eric Thiman's *Path to the Moon* (M051-46114-1; also in Doreen Rao's *We Will Sing!*), Leonard Bernstein's *There Is a Garden* (M051-46816-4), and David Brunner's *Hold Fast Your Dreams* (M051-47123-2).

Keep in mind that these exercises can be uniquely adapted to any musical context and that the improvisational ability of the teacher to adapt and create different *Circle* exercises in each teaching and learning environment is essential.

The Third Foundation

Circle of Sound-in-Rehearsal

The rehearsal techniques and exercises that are suggested in this chapter may be used directly or adapted to any teaching and learning context at any level of vocal instruction. We have selected three different pieces to illustrate how the *Circle of Sound* approach to singing and rehearsal can be effective as a practice-in-action. For each work, we offer specific exercises and techniques. First, however, we will discuss how these techniques can be used generally, throughout each rehearsal and in any musical context. Each of these descriptions applies directly or indirectly to matters of tone quality, vocal intonation, and musical line.

1. The **breathing circle** created for the warm-up or core practice should be maintained in the singer's consciousness as a dynamic image throughout the singing experience. Whenever the singer's pitch lacks tone or resonance, the teacher can invite the singers to shape the imaginary *breath circle* in front of the body. The musical passage lacking resonance can be vocalized with the *breath circle* formation to heighten the singer's awareness of the open throat. When the singers feel the difference, and the teacher hears the difference, the singer can return to standard singing posture. The *breath circle* can be used whenever there is an intonation problem or when the teacher observes that the student is not singing healthfully.

2. The image of the **breathing space** should be developed and maintained systematically over time. It is imperative that the core practice be repeated regularly at the beginning of each lesson or rehearsal so that the student's body and mind has the opportunity to memorize the feeling of the open throat and the muscles have an opportunity to develop and maintain the *singing space*. In rehearsal, the image of the breathing space can be developed and maintained in a variety of ways. First, the teacher should model a singing posture that maximizes the sense of open horizontal and vertical spaces for singing. Second, the circle metaphor can be developed by using the image of the "four directions": north and south (vertical), east and west (horizontal). The image of north and south represent the singer's lifted soft palate and the lowered larynx. The image of east and west represent the singer's widened pharynx (see the circle diagram below). Finally, the circle image can be drawn on the board, or diagrammed for the students to visualize regularly.

3. **Listening space** is essential for beautiful tone and good intonation. Young singers and developing choirs often sing out of tune because they are unable to hear themselves or

Breath Circle (see full exercise on page 28)

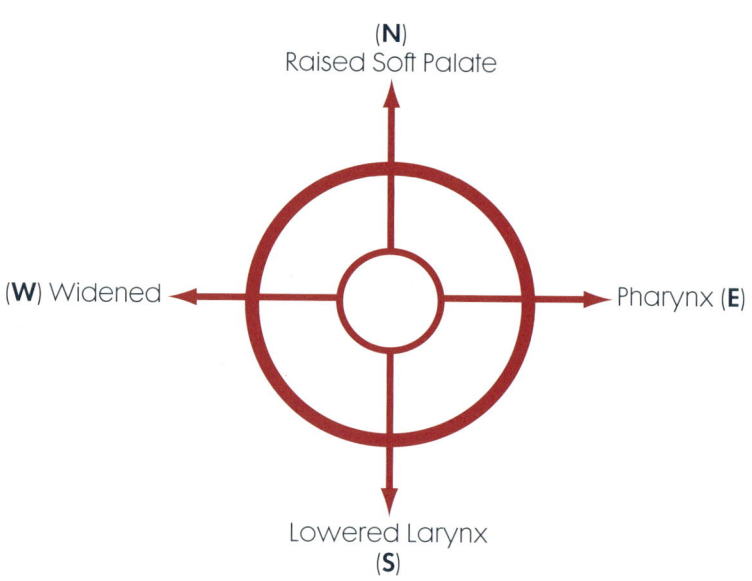

Imagining the vocal tract as the "circle within"

The Third Foundation

others during singing. This is particularly true in ensemble singing. With the limitations of too little technique, singers often bring full weight and volume to all pitches without discrimination. They are unable to lighten the tone or adjust the sung volume to accommodate the melodic character of the line. The ability of the developing singer to listen deeply, to adjust the weight and volume of the tone can be taught effectively through the use of movement and hand motions. Using the natural cadence of the words, the rise and fall of the sung text, the teacher can demonstrate to the singers how to move toward the active syllables (action) and how to "let go" of the inactive syllables (non-action).

This exercise reflects the organic relationship established in the *Circle of Sound* conscious breathing exercises which intentionalize and activate the in-breath and allows the singing tone to take its own course. Using body movements with text, the singers can dance using a combination of step-lift patterns that reflect the time and text patterns established in the music. For example, if a work is in triple meter, it is likely that the text will flow naturally in a *step-lift-lift*, or *heavy-light-light* pattern. Body and hand motions can be improvised to enact the weight and volume of the musical line. The ability of the singer to lighten the tonal weight and to soften the phrase ending is achievable through speech, dance and hand motions, large and small circles improvised in rehearsal. As the body or hand lifts, the tone lifts. As the tone lifts and the volume decreases, the singer will become a more active listener. The ability to listen in singing is directly connected with the ability to vocally create musical contrast from loud to soft, heavy to light, dark to bright, long to short and so on. The more the students enact these musical contrasts through speech and body movement patterns, the faster they will learn to listen deeply in singing.

4. **Singing space** is related to a dynamic concept of vocal acoustics, or the singing environment. There is far more to *singing space* than vocal acoustics alone. While the larynx, pharynx and mouth constitute the vocal tract, and while pitch in singing is manifest in the breath as it moves through the glottis, the singer's tone results in how the singer carries the music from thought to physical expression. Voice scientists and practitioners alike agree that the crucial function essential to the singing voice is the ability to draw the larynx downwards resulting in the maximum stretching and the minimum tensing of the vocal folds. The imaging of *singing space* through the *Circle of Sound* breathing and movement exercises is a natural and organic method of creating the maximum singing space—a primary resource for beautiful tone and in tune singing.

The spaces within the body, particularly the vocal tract or resonance chamber, are only one dimension of what we call *singing space*. More broadly, singers need to develop a conscious relationship with the performance acoustics and rehearsal spaces in which they sing. Helping the singer to develop an understanding of the rehearsal and performance environment requires careful attention. It is important for all singers to recognize the singing environment as an essential part of their vocal potential, as a source of energy, and as an integral contribution to the musical tone. As singers enter into a new room, they should immediately practice the *Circle of Sound* breathing, movement, and vocalization exercises. As they vocalize, they should change the position of their bodies, directing the voice to varying surfaces and spaces around them. They should look north, south, east, and west to explore all four directions of the room. As they sing to all four directions, they will experience a difference in the sound and in the acoustical qualities of their singing. The exploration of the rehearsal or performance environment will increase the singer's sense of *singing space* beyond the comfort of the inner spaces (the vocal tract) to the acoustical complexity of the outer spaces (the performance environment).

There is another important acoustical element that can profoundly impact the singer's sense of his or her *singing space* as well as the beauty and complexity of the singing tone. Beyond the singer's biological-acoustical inner space or vocal tract, and beyond the careful and considered use of environmental acoustics or outer spaces, singers need to pay attention to the acoustic potential that exists between singers. This human or relational acoustic—the connection between

The Third Foundation

singers, can be practiced in rehearsals as the singers sing to one another, face to face, eye to eye. As the singer "bears witness" to the other singer and looks directly into the eyes of the "other," the quality of the musical tone changes quite profoundly. Looking directly at another while you are singing can be an extremely profound experience. The added surface, the direct eye contact, the unmitigated acceptance of the other's tone during vocalization and the energy of a joint enterprise can directly impact the quality of the sung tone and the musical experience of the singer.

The **breath center** is always accessible to the singer. Whenever the singer's tone lacks resonance or when pitch is unstable, the singer should come back "home" to the breath center, placing the left hand on the abdomen. Breathing-in, the singer feels the natural rise of the abdomen. Breathing-out, the singer feels the abdomen fall. The simple connection of bringing one hand to the abdomen "reminds" the singer nonverbally to deepen and lower the breath center.

We use the arched **breath hand** at the face to image the lifted palate and loose tongue during singing. This enactment sends a message to the voice to support and sustain the *singing space* throughout phonation. The circular motion of the *breath hand* enacting the singer's breath movement and *singing space* can be used liberally as an effective technique during rehearsal.

Instructing the singers to prepare the voice with **breathing beats** is used as often as possible to make inhalation a conscious act. *Breathing beats* are used in the core practice as the teacher counts the four *breathing beats* in preparation for vocalization. The same technique can be used in rehearsal context whenever there is time to breath during the musical introduction and between musical phrases. The use of *breathing beats* is an effective tool for teaching students to consciously breathe-in at every opportunity. Focusing on the quality of the inspiration will benefit tone quality and intonation. If the musical introduction or interlude is four beats or longer, the in-breath preparation should be taken in deeply and slowly over a full measure. If the space between phrases is short, the same principle applies, but over a shorter span of time.

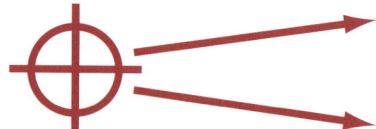

The symbol above is used in *Circle of Sound* vocalization to denote "breathing beats." For definition of "breathing beats," see page 22.

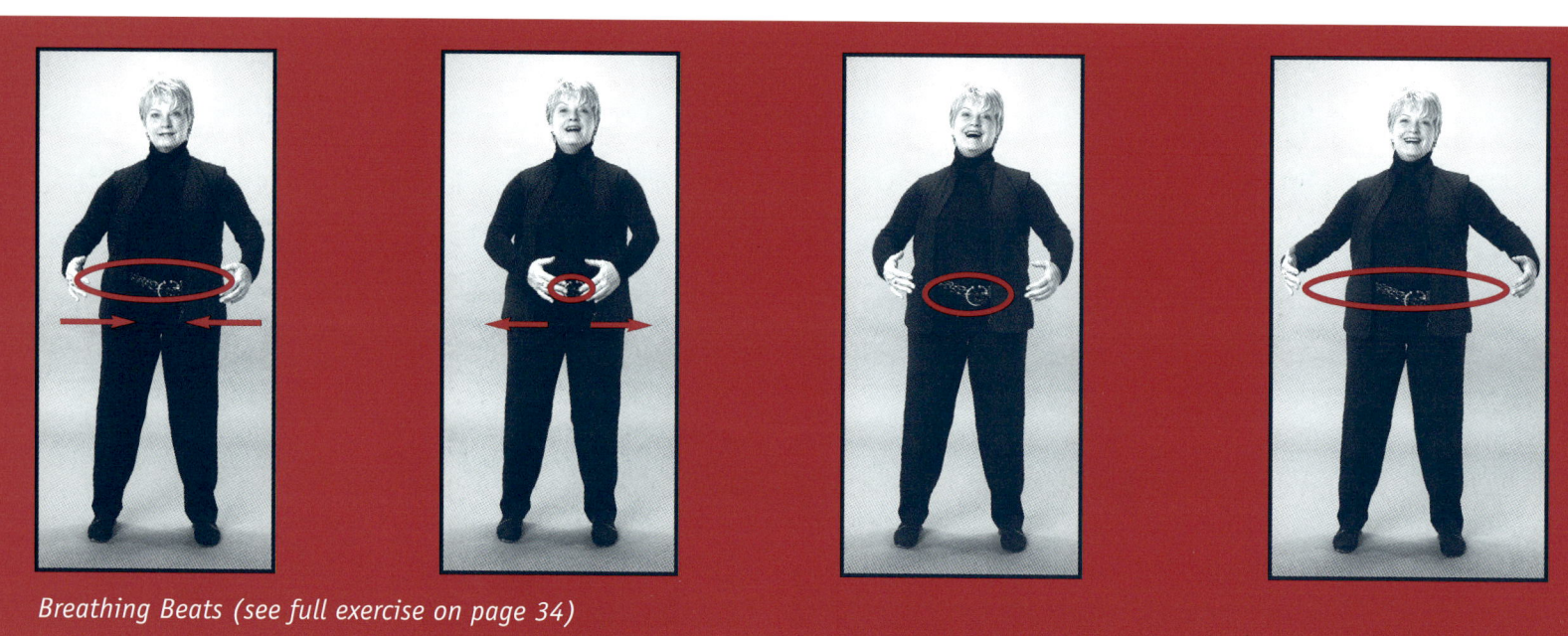

Breathing Beats (see full exercise on page 34)

The Third Foundation

When students are holding music during rehearsals and performances they should be encouraged to bring the printed page into the breath circle and think of the page as an extension of the breath. We call using the music as an extension of breath, a **reading circle**.

Breathing loud, singing soft is a phrase used in the circle practice as a reminder for singers to activate the in-breath and "release" whatever tone results from consciously breathing-in. Often a young singer will try to manipulate the tone or "hold" the tone to compensate for the tone's lack of connection to the breath. If the in-breath is prepared consciously and if the singer *breathes loud*, the tone quality will already be in-formed. When the tone quality is in-formed, it is less likely to require "holding" or artificial manipulation of any kind.

Circle of Sound Practice-in-Action

In lessons or rehearsals it is possible to continually use and adapt the *Circle of Sound Voice Education* practices to achieve a healthier and more informed vocalism. The following rehearsal applications illustrate the use and adaptation of the *Circle of Sound* core practice exercises into the *Circle of Sound* extended practice. The material that follows is limited to a few teaching examples and does not include a complete rehearsal guide. Rehearsal guides and program notes are found on the inside covers of most CME octavos. A complete rehearsal guide to *Path to the Moon* can be found in the choral textbook *We Will Sing!* (See Bibliography.)

THE PEOPLE
Formed a circle round the Fire,
each showing an attentive face
to every other person.

AND THEY SPOKE
each waiting quietly
till the other had finished,
as they had learned to do,
a circle of silent listening
framing the wisdom each contained
Until the wisdom of all was spoken,
contained at last
by the Circle of the People.

—Paula Underwood
"The Walking People"

The Third Foundation

Example 1
Eric Thiman, "Path to the Moon"

1. **Breathing beats-in-time:** This very simple melodic song by English composer Eric Thiman almost sings itself. For solo voice or unison chorus, the lilting compound meter and the long four-bar piano introduction gives the singer ample time to *consciously breathe-in*. In preparation for the first vocal phrase, activate the initial breath preparation by using *breathing beats-in-time* over the full measure of the vocal entrance. To facilitate the five beat in-breath, the teacher can circle a conducting gesture in two while counting out "1, 2, 3, 4, 5." The circle movements and the counting will motivate the singer's conscious breath preparation. The Example 1 Vocalization Exercise on pages 60–61 can help to develop this skill.

2. **Horizontal circle:** In the same musical segment, it is possible to re-enact the *breathing-in-moving-in-time* circle from the *Circle of Sound* core practice. Ask the singer to center the body and form a large *breathing* circle with the hands in front of the body before the piano introduction begins. Begin *breathing-in-moving-in deeply* over two measures (ms 3–4). As the vocalization begins, the singer *sings-out-moves-out slowly* back to the large *breath circle*. The same exercise can be used at the piano interludes in other smaller pieces throughout the piece is neccessary.

3. **Vertical circle:** In the pick-up to measure 5, the octave E♭ interval can be made easier for singers to vocalize when the teacher gestures a large vertical circle to visually motivate the *singing space* required to sing an octave interval. The circle gesture can be created in time and tempo or out of time. The same technique can be used for the vocal entrances throughout the piece as neccessary.

Multiple Circles

4. **Multiple circles:** The singer can create small *circles-in-time* to stimulate conscious breathing and image the open *singing space*. At the conclusion of this song, the passage "to carry me . . ." can be supported by three separate short breaths that can stimulated by making small circles-in-time.

5. **Rainbow arch:** The opening four-bar phrase of each stanza can be sung in a gentle legato style with the help of a circular arch slowly drawn in the air during the vocalization over the full four-bar phrase. A *rainbow arch* made with the singer's *breath hand* moving from left to right through the air stimulates continuous breath flow and helps the singer image the long smooth phrase. Even if the singer must breathe before the phrase is finished, the rainbow arch continues to the end of the phrase.

The full octavo is available from Boosey & Hawkes (M051-46114-1).

The Third Foundation

THE PATH TO THE MOON
for Unison Voices & Piano

Words by
MADELINE C. THOMAS

Music by
ERIC H. THIMAN

long to sail the path to the moon On a deep blue night, when the

wind is cool: A glist-'ning path, that runs out to sea,

© Copyright 1956 by Boosey & Co., Ltd.; Copyright Renewed.
Copyright for all countries. All rights reserved. OCTB6114 Engraved & Printed in U.S.A.

The Third Foundation

Example 1: "Path to the Moon" Vocalization

The Third Foundation

Example 1: "Path to the Moon" Vocalization

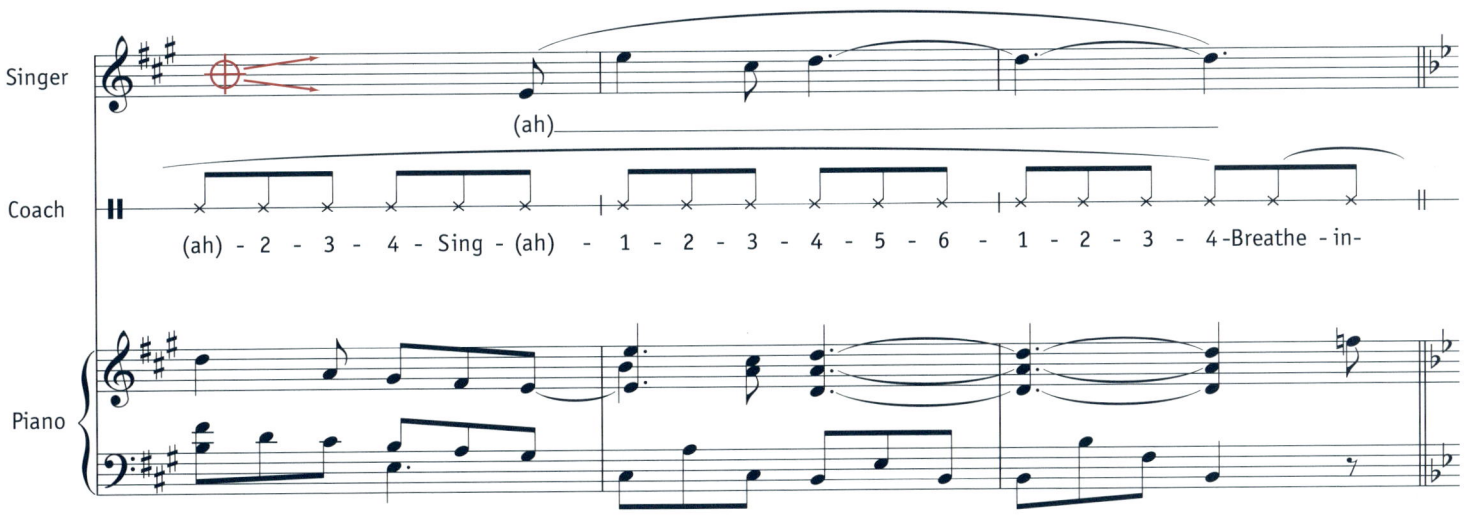

Circle of Sound Voice Education • 61

The Third Foundation

Example 2
David Brunner, "Hold Fast Your Dreams"

1. **Breathing circle**: To prepare the opening phrase, begin the rehearsal with the body in *breath circle* position. Use the measure of the vocal entrance to *breathe-in-move-in slowly* over four beats. *Sing-out* the first note at the peak of the *in-breath* on the text "Hold fast your dreams!" Exercise the use of the breathing circle at the beginning of new phrases to emphasize the importance of conscious breath preparation before each phrase.

2. **Breath crescendo**: There are several places throughout this piece that require the use of crescendo over sustained pitches. To emphasize the breath requirements for the healthy vocalization of a crescendo or a sustained pitch, create the *breath circle* in front of the body, *breathe-in-move-in smiling* and release the tone to the crescendo as the hands move-out back to the large breath circle. This exercise can be extracted and used wherever there is a sustained pitch or wherever there is a crescendo.

3. **Circle shapes**: At phrase endings or cadential points such as measures 28–29, the sustained pitch requires the constant flow of breath through the vowel formation to accomplish beautiful tone and accurate intonation. At such a phrase ending or at any place that requires the singer to maintain an open vowel through a sustained passage, the teacher can use a repeated circular motion with the conducting hand circling the front of her face. This will bring the singer's attention to both the continuous breath flow and the rounded shape of the vowel required to sing the sustained pitch. This technique can be used to sustain the final cadence from measure 43 to the end or any of the passages where the vowel is sustained over an extended pitch.

4. **Singing space**: In this piece the poetic contrast is intensified by the variation in vowel requirements. The cadential texts "heart" and "go" contrast significantly with the word "dreams." It is somewhat easier for a developing singer to sustain the open vowels such as "heart" (hah) or "go" (goh) than it is to sustain a beautiful tone on the word "dreams" (dreems) If the *singing space* is informed through conscious *breathing-in on ah* [a], the brighter tone of the [i] (ee) vowel will have ample space to resonate beautifully without the need to modify the bright vowel to a dark vowel. The Example 2 Vocalization Exercise on pages 64–65 can help to develop this skill.

5. **Breathing Circle**: When the singers are familiar with the pitch requirements, we suggest that a full segment of the piece be vocalized on a single vowel initiated and sustained in the breathing circle posture. Ask the students to center their bodies, soften the knees and create the breath circle position. *Breathing-in-moving-in on* (ah) sing the first full page of music through measure 15 on the (ah) vowel, refreshing the breath whenever it is necessary. This exercise will give developing singers a sense of breath flow, open space, legato line, and resonant tone which they may apply to the same material sung on the text.

The full octavo is available from Boosey & Hawkes (M051-47123-2).

The Third Foundation

*Commissioned by the St. Joseph's Hospital Foundation, for the Tampa Bay Children's Chorus, Averill Summer, Founder-Director
on the occasion of the opening of Tampa Children's Hospital at St. Joseph's, 19 March 1998*

HOLD FAST YOUR DREAMS
for Two-Part Treble Voices & Piano

Text by
Louise Driscoll

Music by
David L. Brunner

© Copyright 1999 by Boosey & Hawkes, Inc.
Copyright for all countries. All rights reserved.

OCTB7123

Engraved & Printed in U.S.A.

The publisher has used its best efforts to clear any copyrighted text that might be included in this work with the relevant owners and to print suitable acknowledgments. If any right owner has not been consulted or an acknowledgment omitted, the publisher offers its apology and will rectify the situation following formal notification.

IMPORTANT NOTICE: The unauthorized copying of the whole or any part of this publication is illegal.

The Third Foundation

Example 2: "Hold Fast Your Dreams" Vocalization

* Singers should breathe in the "ah" of the word "heart" and avoid thinking of the consonant "R."

The Third Foundation

Example 2: "Hold Fast Your Dreams" Vocalization

Circle of Sound Voice Education • 65

The Third Foundation

Example 3

Leonard Bernstein, "There is a Garden"

1. **Reading circle:** As the singer approaches the learning of Bernstein's dramatic and emotionally complex song, the octavo should be held with two hands as part of the *breathing circle* in front of the body. Linking the printed page with the breathing process can help to improve the quality of the singing tone as the student is reading the score. Bringing the printed page into the *breathing circle* creates a more organic connection between singing and reading.

2. **Breathing circle:** In the chorus section that starts for the first time at measure 28, the descending fifth in measure 29 on the word "gar-den" can be problematic. The descending [g] often sounds flat due to the weight of the tone at the end of the phrase. If the singer is instructed to maintain the singing space with the large *breath circle* formation in the front of the body during the singing of that phrase, a natural "lift" or lightness enters the descending interval and the [g] will likely stay in tune. Showing the *breath circle* during singing reminds the soft palate to stay high during phonation.

3. **Breath space:** In the rehearsal of this song both the verse and the chorus need to be vocalized on the breath. To give singers a dramatic sense of the difference between singing on the breath and singing without breath, compare and contrast singing a phrase with the body in a standard posture, without conscious breathing and without the breath space preparation. Have the singers sing and listen to one phrase sung without conscious breathing and then have the singers sing and listen to the same phrase sung with conscious breathing in the breath space. The results of this comparison will be dramatic and the students will like the way they feel and the way they sound when they are singing *on the breath*.

4. **Breathing-in-moving-in:** In the opening verse section of this song, the recitative style of its dramatic content requires concentrated diction. This style of vocalization is often challenging for the developing singer. There is a tendency to forget to breath due to the short clips of text without much time to breathe between phrases. Ask the students to form a *breath circle* by *breathing-in-moving-into* the circle position. Sing four bars of the verse in the *breath circle* position. Sing the same four bars without the *breath circle* to compare and contrast the difference in tone between the two examples. *On the breath*, the text will communicate much more dramatically.

5. **Rainbow arch:** To create legato phrasing in the chorus sections of this song, ask the singers to create a *rainbow arch* prepared on the in-breath and shaped with the right hand moving from left to right throughout the full length of the phrase.

The full octavo is available from Boosey & Hawkes (M051-46816-4).

The Third Foundation

THERE IS A GARDEN
from TROUBLE IN TAHITI
for Unison Treble Voices & Piano

Words & Music by
LEONARD BERNSTEIN

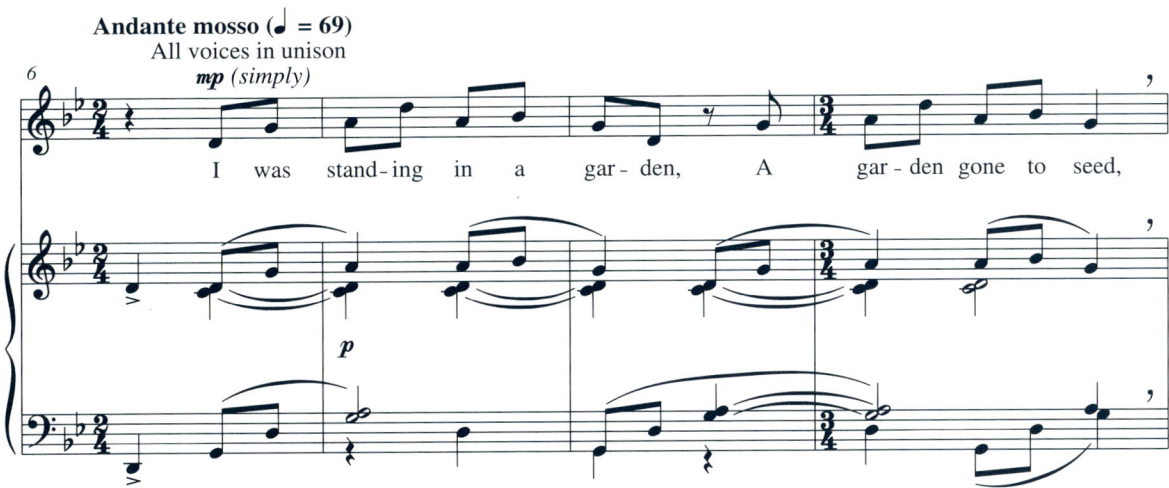

Copyright © 1953 by Leonard Bernstein; Copyright Renewed.
Leonard Bernstein Music Publishing Company LLC, Publisher
Boosey & Hawkes, Inc., Sole Agent
International Copyright Secured. All rights reserved.   OCTB6816   Engraved & Printed in U.S.A. 1998.

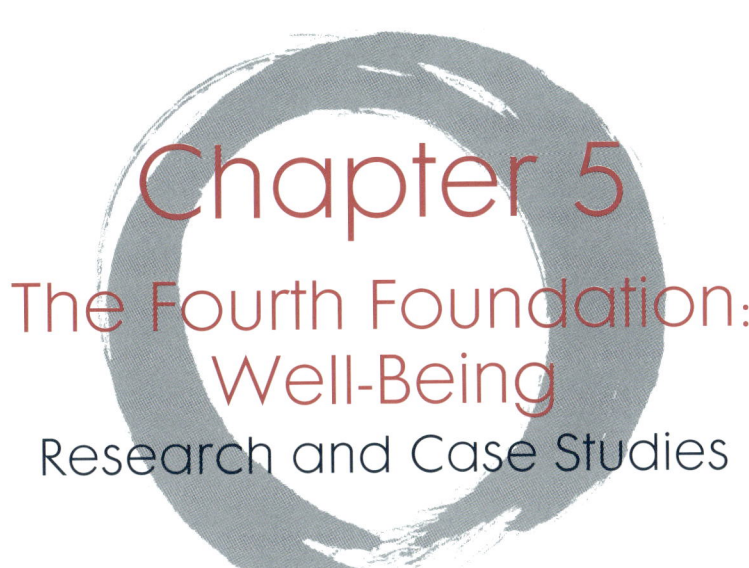

Chapter 5
The Fourth Foundation: Well-Being
Research and Case Studies

At the very least, *Circle of Sound Voice Education* as a contemplative approach to singing can reduce stress, increase concentration, and improve singing tone. Moreover, there is mounting evidence that this approach to vocal performance may also contribute significantly to improved health and emotional well-being. The research on meditation tells us that through regular meditation practice, the brain is reoriented from a stressful fight-or-flight mode to one of acceptance, a shift that increases contentment.[1] It is not surprising that similar contemplative approaches to stress reduction and concentration are being developed and used in schools, hospitals, law firms, government buildings, corporate offices, and prisons.

Circle of Sound Voice Education is a way of reaching out across disciplines and cultures to come to a deeper understanding of singing as well-being. This cross-cultural and interdisciplinary journey of understanding links voice education with its social and emotional potential to teach everyday skills like self-awareness, self-control, and the management of anger, fear, and anxiety—desirable teachings for life. We know through years of field testing and lived experience that the *Circle of Sound* approach to singing reduces singers' anxiety and increases singers' joy, enthusiasm, and good will. In this approach, singing is a medium for *becoming!*—a way of singing that constitutes a way of being.[2]

Friends and colleagues often ask us about the origin of our experiences with the *Circle of Sound* contemplative approach to voice education. Responding to these probing questions, this chapter offers a sampling of supporting perspectives including personal narrative, selected research, case study, and field testing reports. We hope that the following discussions will enrich the reader's understanding of the "education-as-life" value embodied in the *Circle of Sound* contemplative approach to singing.

A Singer's Story
Doreen Rao's Personal Narrative

Recently a journalist interviewed me to find out what it was in my background that led me to pursue a career in choral music. He was curious about my commitment to multicultural music and somewhat cautious about my interdisciplinary way of thinking about choral musical experience. I sensed he could not decide whether I was on the fringe or the forefront of my profession. I did not tell him that for the better part of my professional life, I bought into the eurocentric notion of beauty for its own sake and that my professional reputation came largely from the ability to craft high level professional performances for the sake of "music education" as truth and beauty. What is not in my published biography that would explain the emergence of this cross-cultural, cross-disciplinary alternative approach to singing? I guess it could be called *life*.

Circle of Sound Voice Education • 69

The Fourth Foundation

I was raised on the European classics, Beethoven, Brahms, Mendelssohn, and lots of opera! My mother was a singer, a dramatic lyric soprano who refused any popular music in our house. Lucky for me, my father worked at Chicago's famous London House, home to jazz greats Ella Fitzgerald, Oscar Peterson, Duke Ellington, and Louis Armstrong. My brother and I visited the London House once a month where we sat right next to these great musicians. That's only the beginning of what might be considered a life of *living diversity*.

My formal education in music began as a pianist and later voice studies. At the University of Illinois, I had the great fortune to study with Harold Decker and Colleen Kirk—two of America's most generous, compassionate, and caring choral music educators. Dr. Decker was always premiering new works. Dr. Kirk always cared. At the University's School of Music, the curriculum did not separate the study of music performance from of music education. We did not isolate music education from music.

In Chicago, I sang professionally and taught general music in the public schools. I wanted to teach all the students in my classes to sing, but the administration determined that choral singing could only be offered before or after school. So the school district bussed 278 of 300 junior high students in and out, everyday, before and after school. Obviously the students wanted to sing in choirs! Then there was the wonderful Glen Ellyn Children's Chorus, where singing great literature *was* music education.

My doctoral studies with Bennett Reimer at Northwestern University in music education philosophy were complemented by the richness of my performance career as Margaret Hillis's assistant conductor with the Chicago Symphony Chorus. Reading philosophy was not always easy while raising a family, conducting a children's chorus, and meeting the challenges of a personal life. But it was during those busy and challenging years that I developed the *Choral Music Experience* performance approach to music education and during that period of graduate research that I crafted a language to put to those features which distinguished a *performance approach* from the concept-based, *elements of music* approach used in general music education.

I had always believed that the value of musical experience was embodied in musical "making and doing," or *techne*, as the Greeks called it. I also believed that singing and vocal performance might eventually be understood as a dynamic and intelligent form of *musical knowing* or *non-verbal knowledge*. My struggle to understand musical performance as a form of knowledge, as body, mind, and feeling was partially resolved in my Ph.D. dissertation guided by Dr. Reimer.

In 1988 I defended my dissertation: *Craft, Singing Craft and Musical Experience*. This research shows how the physical, spiritual, creative, and cognitive aspects of singing serve as a multidimensional, non-verbal form of procedural knowledge or "thinking-in-action." In 1993, my choral textbook *We Will Sing!* drew from this research to develop a vocal performance approach for classroom music. In his 1995 text *Music Matters: A New Philosophy of Music Education*, Canadian music educator David Elliott develops what he calls his praxial view of music teaching and learning using the term "musicianship" to elaborate and extend my "craft" thesis. Readers of these texts will find a certain resonance in the intellectual compatibility of these ideas.

For the past six years, crossing over to research in anthropology, the contemplative arts, MusicMedicine, feminism, and theology has broadened my understanding of how singing experience in-forms our bodies, minds, and souls. A quote from Orpingalik, an Inuit leader of the Netsilik People, best expresses the nature of singing: *"How many songs I have I cannot tell you. I keep no count of such things. There are so many occasions in one's life when a joy or a sorrow is felt in such a way that the desire comes to sing; and so I only know that I have many songs. All my being is a song, and I sing as I draw breath."*[3]

I have little doubt that the realities of our world today will continue to inform our understanding of singing as a form of well-being, perhaps more so than ever before.

The Fourth Foundation

Research in Singing

The subject of singing has engaged the minds of philosophers and musicians throughout history. In his preface to George Rhau's *Symphoniae Incundae*, German theologian Martin Luther explains:

> *Philosophers have labored to explain the marvelous instrument of the human voice: how can the air projected by the light movement of the tongue and an even lighter movement of the throat produce such an infinite variety and articulation of the voice? And how can the voice sound forth so powerfully? Philosophers for all their labor cannot find the explanation . . . none of them has yet been able to define or demonstrate the original components of the human voice. They marvel, but they do not understand.*[4]

We have come a long way from the time of Martin Luther, but we still have fundamentally important questions to answer. Research in singing has treated the voice almost exclusively from a scientific, or biological-acoustical perspective. Few studies consider the voice holistically as a multidimensional phenomenon embodying its biological, emotional, and spiritual nature.[5] While early definitions of voice suggest both an *inner voice* (the voice of God or spirit) and an *outer voice* (the voice of reason), voice teaching often focuses exclusively on the manipulation of the vocal apparatus in the production, control, and coordination of pitch.

The separation of the biological dimension from the psycho-spiritual dimension of singing in contemporary voice research and practice contrasts significantly with Aristotle's classical view of singing, in which the soul and the body constitute a single substance. Aristotle's thinking intuitively connects the organic, biological dimension of voice to its psycho-spiritual dimension. In singing, the voice as body and spirit functions as one inseparable, single phenomenon. Unfortunately, Descartes's seventeenth-century philosophy, "I think, therefore I am" (*cogito ergo sum*), took westerners on a three-hundred year detour away from the bodily and spiritual forms of knowing into the land of cognition and so-called objectivity. Theologian and philosopher Thomas Merton said that the concept of *cogito ergo sum* ("I think, therefore I am") was the declaration of an alienated being.[6] Personally, I suspect Descartes never sang in a good choir.

Scientific Research

There is new evidence to suggest that vocalization is connected to an area of the brain called periaquaductal grey (PAG). This part of the brain is known to link vocalization with emotional expression. It is reported that PAG is located in the "unconscious" part of the midbrain area and is influenced by sensory input from the respiratory system and the larynx during vocalization. This research suggests that the connections between brain, larynx, respiratory function, and emotional expression should be addressed in voice education by emotional rather than cognitive means.[7]

Concerning the healing powers of breathing and movement in singing, a strong link between music and healing has been developed by musician-neuroscientist Manfred Clynes, a leader in the study of emotional responses to music. Dr. Clynes's many publications on music and healing address the link between thought and movement as a direct crossing of the mind-body barrier. Given that modern medicine has certainly demonstrated a connection between emotional and physical health, Clynes's many writings suggest that singing and music are a key to the promotion of health and well-being.[8]

The most in-depth scientific research pertinent to the benefits of breathing meditation on health and well-being comes from the advances in medical technologies that are able to measure the long term results of contemplative practices on the brain. The Mind and Life Institute in Boulder, Colorado, is working with His Holiness the Dalai Lama and a community of experts throughout the world to investigate the impact of

The Fourth Foundation

meditation on our thoughts and emotions. Neuroscientist Richard Davidson at the University of Wisconsin has spent his career studying depression and anxiety. He is also studying happiness and mindfulness. Davidson's work measures the effect of mindfulness practice on beginners. With Jon Kabit-Zinn,[9] the study found that through short periods of breathing meditation participants had reduced anxiety, improved immune systems, and increased activity in the area of the brain associated with positive emotions such as joy, enthusiasm, and good will.[10]

Examining the physiological and psychological effects of singing on children and youth as a way of understanding how singing can promote health, choral music educator Heather Eyerly is currently working in the fields of psychophysiology and immunophysiology. In this area related to MusicMedicine, researchers are investigating the physiological and psychological responses to musical experience as a means for understanding how singing affects the singer's health. Professor Eyerly is researching how the effects of the *Circle of Sound Voice Education* approach to singing might elicit an improved immune response that will promote the health of children singing in choirs.[11]

Throughout the history of voice education, teachers have known instinctively that emotion rules vocalization, and that the singer's sense of emotional well-being is central to her ability to sing. That scientific evidence has only recently started to support what teachers of singing have practiced instinctively throughout time is a small but important step forward.

Swedish voice scientist Johan Sundberg contemplates the relationship of singing and feeling, lamenting that our profession knows very little or nothing about the emotional aspects of singing experience. He concludes: "let us hope that future research will fill this curious and challenging gap."[12]

The development of the singing voice is an ongoing, life-long pursuit. And while teachers can expect that in the best situations their students will make impressive progress during a given time frame, neither brilliant pedagogy, personal empathy, or an understanding heart alone can protect the sensitive and often gifted voice student from the "inner noises" of personal fear and anxiety. Often our students cannot begin to hear the teachers' instruction, much less listen deeply to their own bodies as a primary source of understanding. The pathways of learning are blocked or unopened. It would seem that fear and anxiety are the constant companions of many young singers.

Current research in vocal physiology and vocal acoustics confirms that the quality of the singer's breathing affects the quality of phonation, the loudness and softness of tone, and the pitch and intensity of tone. Sundberg and other voice scientists tell us that breathing is the most important physiological aspect of singing. Our own research suggests that it is the singer's conscious breathing, the quality of breathing-in and breathing-out that unites mind with body, allowing for the merging of vocal action and musical awareness. Yet, while breathing may be the single most important feature of singing, teachers and conductors regularly witness students *not* breathing or holding their breath. Is it possible that modern life and learning environments in today's world have taught students to stop breathing?

Psycho-Spiritual Studies

I have found that both medical and musical research in cross-cultural sound healing offers fresh perspectives that logically and holistically embrace the mind-body-spirit nature of singing experience. In the medicine, psychology, and music-therapy fields, singing and ritual chant is being celebrated as an alternative form of therapy in treating mental and physical illness. Physicians and music therapists suggest that singing is a way to release tension, center the self, charge the brain, and stimulate bone conduction. The toning and humming forms of vocalization that have been used historically by Zen Buddhist monks and indigenous healers are now being investigated and practiced by western physicians and music therapists to diagnose and treat patients.

The Fourth Foundation

Dr. Pat Moffitt Cook, Director of the Open Ear Center for Music and Healing and editor of the *Open Ear Journal*, has pioneered research in cross-cultural music and healing. Drawing from science and culture, medicine and mysticism, Pat shows how singing, chanting, and vocalization can alter the physical, mental and emotional posture of the body and how these impact physical and mental health.

Psychotherapists have engaged in research on the use of singing, listening, and playing in psychoanalysis. Jungian analyst Patricia Warming's studies linking religion, psychology, and singing included an interesting report on the work of concert pianist and music therapist Margaret Tilley, reported earlier in this text.

Warming and her Jungian colleagues are interested in the therapeutic use of vocalization and vocal performance—the experience of hearing/feeling musically through skin-and-bone-conducted vibrations. These colleagues continue to suggest that singing is a form of respiratory yoga, producing sound frequencies that charge the cortex and result in pronounced physiological effects that contribute to the health of the singer.

In a study related to consciousness and group resonance in musical performance, physician Stuart Silverman developed an experiment in New Mexico dealing with the emotional issues of fear and anxiety related to singing Handel's *Messiah*. Using traditional and alternative strategies, including using conscious breathing, movement, and imagery during rehearsals, Silverman sought to create a safe and unified rehearsal environment for a group of professional musicians. The performer evaluations described the experience as powerful and moving. One of the musicians said, "Learning to stay in the present moment . . . will be helpful in many areas." "Staying in touch with one's body . . . technical matters seem to have receded in importance."[13] This study and other similar work suggests that the use of contemplative approaches to singing, including breathing and movement in rehearsal and lessons can be valuable artistically and therapeutically.

Research in Education

Current literature on music psychology and music education focuses on the formation of consciousness through musical performance. Distinguished University of Chicago scholar Mihaly Csikszentmihalyi has authored numerous studies on the creative process of artists at work. He has closely observed musicians' intense and total involvement as they struggled to bring life to the music.

Csikszentmihalyi describes the characteristics of artistic experience, including deep concentration, joy, emotion, and self-transcendence as *autotelic experience*, popularly known as the merging of action and awareness or *flow*.[14] Described as the psychology of optimal experience, *flow* is the result of the artist's ability to focus, to concentrate deeply, and thus give order to consciousness.

In *flow*, understood as a quality of musical experience, preoccupation with the past or the future disappears. There is a sense of well-being without the feeling of needing to be in control. Awareness is at the core of the *flow* experience—it is complete absorption that results from deep concentration and understanding.

There is an interesting correlation between Csikszentmihalyi's research on the characteristics of creativity with the thirteenth-century Zen master Dogen's teachings which say that in those moments when the world is experienced with the whole of one's body and mind, the senses are joined, the self is opened, and life discloses an intrinsic richness and joy in being.[15]

In his text *Philosophical Perspectives on Music Education*, Wayne D. Bowman develops a diverse and pluralistic account of musical experience.[16] In his rich description of "music as experienced,"[17] and in commentary on Eleanor Stubley's elaboration on "the transformative powers of musical performance,"[18] (or how body and music inform each other in the act of music making), Bowman suggests that music education research seriously neglects the body's role in music and

The Fourth Foundation

music education. Bowman and Stubley suggest that to understand singing, or any other act of music making, it is necessary to get inside the musical field where performance actions occur, "a field that is at once physical, mental, and spiritual."[19] Singing then is just such a musical field, a dynamic and personal field where students can find ways of being in the body and being in the sound.

John P. Miller, author of *The Holistic Teacher* and University of Toronto Professor at the Ontario Institute for Studies in Education, requires students in his graduate courses to practice conscious breathing meditation at the beginning of each meeting. Professor Miller has found a strong link between meditation practice and teaching and learning effectiveness.

From years of data collection, Professor Miller was able to identify five main themes that arise out of educators' use of breathing meditation. These themes included the ability to witness or observe one's own feelings, the ability to become a better listener, the ability to sense interrelatedness and connectedness, the ability to be still and enjoy increased attention in one's daily life, and the ability to be alone and enjoy one's own company. [20]

The amount of research that supports *Circle of Sound Voice Education* as an artistic, educational, and healthful approach to singing is too vast to report in this book. As the reader approaches the case studies reported next, it may help to keep in mind the themes that emerge from this research in science and education with respect to the Four Foundations of *Circle of Sound*: the development of awareness, mindfulness, deep listening, and well-being.

These themes include the physical, emotional, psychological, and social benefits of this contemplative approach to singing. Physically, as the singer breathes-in, the inspiration pushes stale air out of the body reducing stress, improving circulation, and energizing and relaxing the body. Emotionally, *Circle of Sound* relieves anxiety and the symptoms of depression, releases emotion and changes moods. Psychologically, *Circle of Sound* empties the mind of mental clutter, increases self-esteem, eases loneliness, and uplifts the spirit. Socially, *Circle of Sound* brings people together to form communities, creates the opportunity for intimacy, and allows for communication without words.[21]

As you read the *Circle of Sound* Case Studies, remember these themes and take note of the many benefits this contemplative approach to singing can have for you and your students.

Circle of Sound Case Studies

Mindfulness Works!
Jennifer Hand
Phillips Exeter Academy

In short, mindfulness works! It works as both a meditative/reflective practice and as an entry to deep concentration and focus. I've used it with sixth and seventh graders (co-ed and single sex groups), and high schoolers. I have also used it with the choral society with which I sing. Mindfulness has had a positive effect on each of these very different groups.

For the high school singers, it was a way of coming together and pausing quietly—a welcome respite in the middle of a hectic day. As the girls grew more accustomed to the practice, it became a way for me to reach their sound and also for the singers to find each other's sound. The effect on the tone of the choir was remarkable. It invited more personal singing from them and the confidence to take risks with their voices.

Mindfulness provides a rare moment of quiet and a focused group activity for the middle school students, too. The students follow a tight schedule, with next to no free periods in a nine-period day that starts at 8:30 a.m. Afternoon activities begin at 3:20 p.m. and frequently don't wrap up until 5:30 p.m. When students come to my class, they often come directly from lunch or recess and are very wound up. A few minutes of mindfulness gets the choir, if not entirely, at least partially back on track.

The Fourth Foundation

I had the opportunity to conduct a rehearsal for my [adult] choral society, and since the first thing I wanted to work on was Holst's *Psalm 86*, I thought mindfulness would invite the right singing spirit. Like most earnest amateurs, our singers have a tendency to overproduce. So, very slowly and carefully I took them through the three stages of the practice: breathing, to movement, to vocalization. I had very few non-participants in a group of 80. Cool! So when we began the Holst and I immediately received a sound which was overproduced, I merely reminded them of the simple sound which they had attained in the warm up. The change in the tone was immediate. Moreover, as we begin to rehearse the Pärt *Te Deum*, I kept using key words such as "circles," "space," and "release" to guide them to a sound that was natural, not manufactured. When asked if they felt the difference or heard the difference, there were nods of assent. That was encouraging.

I reread my Choral Music Experience Institute notes frequently to make sure I never stray too far from the essence of the practice. I am reminded to stay grounded and anchored, to let my breath carry the tone out of my body and into the macro-circles or space inside my body, in the chest, the back, and the throat.

Circle of Sound Voice Education Amazes Me
Jennifer Hand

Circle of Sound continues to amaze me. One of the ideas that struck me is that music is circular art. The artist/performer gives out his or her emotion through the music to the audience, and the audience gives something back to the performer in response. When I read this I thought, "Okay, so this macro-breath/movement exercise represents not just what's going on physiologically, but emotionally as well".

It's the big picture, and somehow my students need to learn that too.

In my experience as a chorister, music was always about my relationship to the score, with the conductor, my fellow singers, and my audience. Concerts felt somewhat unfulfilled if my parents weren't in the front row and my non-musical friends weren't there as well. I sang to them as much as I sang for myself. Clearly what I was experiencing, in my own way and in my own space, was the natural organic way of starting to sing. My conductor always helped me find my sound from the inside and never imposed technique from the outside. I always said I was most myself—giving and sharing—when singing.

Now as the teacher, I often doubt how I can give my students those feelings.

However, I am learning that the first stage of breathing meditation, (stopping, calming, and recognizing) does indeed lead to concentration. With concentration (and some gimmicks!) my students are becoming more insightful about their own work. When they begin to assess themselves on a job done well (or not), they demonstrate their personal understanding. And as their teacher, I learn more about what they know about themselves.

Furthermore, when I set the stage for their learning, or give them a platform on which they can experiment, they end up leading themselves to see musical relationships. This helps them take responsibility for their own learning. As a result, they are given an experience that pleases them and one that they want to duplicate and share with others.

Using "Mindfulness"
Marguerite McCormick
Founder and Artistic Director of
San Antonio Children's Chorus

My introduction to mindfulness was at the Choral Music Experience Institute in Arvika, Sweden. Dr. Rao began each day with readings and examples of mindfulness for singers and conductors/teachers. Noticing the positive influences on my own focus and well-being, I realized that this approach could also have truly beneficial effects on our young singers.

The Fourth Foundation

Before the start of the season, I shared my notes and examples with our staff and encouraged them to use the mindfulness exercises at the beginning of each rehearsal. They were intrigued by the possibilities, not only for vocal development but also for focusing our youngsters' concentration in an efficient manner. Beginning with the season's first rehearsal, the singers in each of our four choirs were introduced to the mindfulness exercises. We could see and hear differences in the children from their first experience with the mindfulness approach. Many embraced the ideas and suggestions readily, some took more time to adjust to it, but they all participated!

Children's Chorus of San Antonio has approximately 150 singers (ages 9–18) in four choirs. The youngsters come from all over the San Antonio metropolitan area and outlying communities. Our regular rehearsals begin at 4:20 p.m. at a location that is a ten to fifteen minute drive for some while others have a 30- to 60-minute commute. Traffic congestion, unexpected delays at school, and family emergencies all take their toll on our singers' rehearsal readiness. And sometimes a child has simply had a bad day. Another reason that mindfulness appealed to our staff is that we are always looking for ways to help our youngsters feel and understand the connection between breath support and the singing voice.

We began by using the settling and calming and the first of the physical/vocal exercises, then added a new physical/vocal exercise each week until we had the full series of three. All singers were told that if they came in to rehearsal after mindfulness had started, they should enter as quietly as possible and pick up the exercise with the rest of the group. This was especially helpful with our youngest or most inexperienced children because it helped them focus immediately on the business at hand.

At the end of the previous season, we had graduated a large number of high school seniors and also lost some of our more experienced singers for other reasons. So younger, less experienced, singers made up about half of the membership in our upper choirs as we began the next season. For these youngsters, in particular, mindfulness was a wonderful tool in helping them develop vocal confidence and greater expertise. These two upper choirs had to prepare two different performances with the San Antonio Symphony and a concert at the Round Top Festival Institute, as well as our regular concert series, all in the fall. I found that I could use mindfulness to great advantage just prior to our performances by having the children "image" the physical sensations of the mindfulness exercises and apply that to their vocal production. Even if the warm-up room was cramped and crowded, this idea really worked well. Mindfulness also helped these particular singers maintain poise, focus, and vocal readiness on the concert stage.

Our novice singers have simply accepted mindfulness as the way we begin our rehearsals. It has worked with youngsters who have serious attention problems, as well as the child who "spaces out" occasionally. What the staff noticed early in the season was that the singers in the two lower choirs developed a warmer, richer tone quality, and they learned to apply what they heard and felt in mindfulness warm-ups to their season repertoire.

We will continue to use the mindfulness philosophy and exercises next season, eager to build on the benefits we could see and hear.

I Am Delighted with the Results
Megan Marshall
Conductor, Glen Ellyn Children's Chorus

In my experience, the practice of t'ai chi becomes a useful tool when applied to singing, because it unites the mind, breath, body, and voice. I do not feel I have to be a t'ai chi expert or even a regular practitioner. If I did, I would not have dared apply the ideas to my teaching. As it is, I have felt able to use what I have learned about t'ai chi with my students.

I have never told my students the ideas come from t'ai chi.

The use of conscious breathing and the accompanying phrases is just as helpful for me as it is for my singers! I always

The Fourth Foundation

invite them to close their eyes, or if they would prefer, just lower them. Most of them work well with me. However, at the start of the conscious breathing, some singers find it hard to focus (a few always giggle!), but by the time I get to the "smiling/relaxing" phrase, they seem to be able to put their giggly energy into the smile. I am hoping that as the practice becomes more routine, they will find the focus from the beginning.

So far, I have only used one of the three main vocal exercises (in addition to the conscious breathing exercise). The vocal exercise I have used is the descending five-step "nu." The combination of breath and movement has been very helpful for my choir to find a strong singing stance, albeit subconsciously. Their posture is greatly improved, and they can maintain good posture for longer stretches of the rehearsal. I noticed this right from the first rehearsal.

Sometimes I adapt the exercises. I take the same movements for the "na" vocalization, but ask the singers not to sing. Instead, I ask them to practice a basic cool air sip as the arms move inward and sustain a "ts" on the breath as the arms move back open. Because there is no vocalization, I can move away from the piano and gauge the quality of their movement.

I periodically use the phrase, "find your center." (This is much more positive and productive than saying, "you're standing like a lazy middle-school student waiting in the lunch line"). The singers seem to grasp that concept well, especially when there's a model in front of them—be it a student who seems very well centered, or me. They know that this warm-up takes discipline and that they can't be lazy. At first they seemed surprised that I could be so particular about such a "simple" movement/vocalization.

Recently, I asked some of my students to reflect on the new warm-up in a journal. I phrased the question in the following way: "The warm-up, 'nah' with the arm movement is important to your understanding of yourself as a Full Singer/Complete Singer. How has this warm-up helped you? What has it taught you?"

Some of the student responses were:

The arm movements help me to breathe correctly while singing.

This warm-up has taught me to sing out, keep my posture, and move to the rhythm of the music.

The warm-up has helped me with my stance and with my breathing. It has taught me to stand and sing without lifting my shoulders as I breath or sing out.

It has taught me to relax my jaw and have more space in my mouth.

It helped me to sing louder and sing out more.

It helps by making me breathe better and by bringing my voice out. It has taught me to hold the long notes.

It has taught me to raise my volume and open my jaw so I can sing the full phrase.

It helps me get from one note to another without taking a breath in between and it gives me better posture.

It helps me because it makes me sing better. It opens my mind and relaxes me. It has taught me how to sing clearly and open my mouth naturally.

The Fourth Foundation

Even though I feel that I am still very much a novice, I am delighted with the results both in my own practice and in the effect it has had on my teaching. In particular, the reflections from my students really pleased me, because I didn't tell them to sing out more or to have better posture because of this exercise. I believe the practice has helped the singers to be aware of the muscular requirements for good singing posture.

Wow! This Stuff Works!
Bill Perison
Author
(from a letter to Doreen Rao, January 1998)

Well, all I can say is "Wow! This stuff works!" I had a session last night with A.M.'s community choir. There were only about fifteen people because of a snowstorm (three inches paralyzed this place!).

Anyway, just the stretching routine did wonders.

I started out with a stretching warm-up and then *wuji* standing posture with melting a warm light or smile down the front, back, and core or center of the body. This is a wonderful centering practice. If the singers practice it regularly, they would be able to access their breath center instantly. The Chinese call this "Sung" and in t'ai chi, a state of softness—yet with strength or structure. ("Steel wrapped in cotton.")

I then used the ball exercise to establish the space of the breath circle. Each singer worked with a partner gently pushing on the arms to see how relaxed the arms could be whilst maintaining the strength and structure of "ball" (the breath circle). The singers were all mothers, so I used the analogy of an infant's legs when the child is beginning to stand or bounce on the lap: The way the legs have a "softness" and yet at the same time "incredible strength." This analogy helped a number of women in the choir. We also found it helpful to raise our arms too high to see how little strength there is when we are out of our sphere. This exercise demonstrated the benefit of engaging the entire skeletal muscle structure to achieve the desired effect.

Following this movement, the singers breathed within the circle and sang an "Ah." The sound was open and had a very resonant tone. I think the singers (and their conductor) were surprised at the ease with which they sang. We didn't push the envelope in terms of range, but on an octave leap vocal exercise, the choir sang to F# and no one—including the altos—thought it was at all difficult. It really isn't difficult, but I think some singers see a high note and think, "Wow! this is going to be tough," and then it is tough. I used to do that when playing the trumpet. I solved the problem by giving up the trumpet!

I also asked the choir to sing whilst standing in a tight, stiff position to see how it felt and sounded. They didn't like it, compared with the open feeling of the more relaxed position.

We worked for fifty minutes and the choir was glowing by the end. I will go back next week when the snow is gone to work the *whole* group. The biggest message of the night was how important it is to engage the whole body when singing. One singer said that although she'd been told over the years to "use your whole body," she had never been able to do so until now. I suspect that she was only using a larger percentage of her body in singing this time than she was before, but she's on the way.

There is much more to work out, discover, and tie together, but I am very excited about this work. It feels so, so right!

What Are Your Passions?
Tamara Schupmann
Conductor, Singer, Teacher
Spokane, Washington

The first question Doreen Rao put to us at Choral Music Experience Institute was, "Who are you and what are your passions?" "Music" was my answer.

And so we began, and the sea storms came and I asked myself, "What will come from this experience?"

The Fourth Foundation

There were many "storms" that week which spoke to me in powerful ways, particularly the "storm" of "the breath circle."

Concentration on the quality of the intake and release of the breath and related movements to those activities had a profound effect on me. Moreover, the effect on the children of the choir in residence was remarkable.

As a singer, I already understood the need for "proper" breath management. But it was the singleness of thought, intention, and attention, so beautifully and skillfully demonstrated by Doreen and Bill, which gave the breath the importance it deserves.

I'm excited about the possibilities of focusing children on this thoughtful and effective way of breathing. With more thorough and passionate teaching, I look forward to igniting the potential sound in my singers, as it did with the young artists in residence at the CME Institute for Choral Teacher Education. My hope is that the passion *Circle of Sound Voice Education* inspired in me will become a part of my being forever and alter the landscape of my conducting as an educator, artist, and peacemaker.

Chapter 6
Closing the Circle
Singing in the World Today

This chapter introduces a selected repertoire of stretching, rooting, and movement forms that can enhance the quality of the student's singing experience. Singing is a form of practical intelligence exercised in action. Singers develop the ability to respond and to change things based on their feelings, perceptions, and consciousness accessed through the body, in the body. This skillful gesture called singing can be thought of as a form of *bodily wisdom*.

Like all forms of wisdom, the wisdom of the body develops slowly and requires regular attention. Traditional exercises generally stress *doing* something to improve vocal tone or ease a performance tension. *Circle of Sound* encourages the cultivation of non-doing, or *wu-wei*, as a knowledgeable, *effortless effort* that can be cultivated through regular practice. *Non-doing* means letting things be and allowing them to unfold in their own way. Effortless activity happens at moments in music, dance and sports at the highest levels of performance. The ability to"let" the voice sing, to "let" the performance unfold beyond technique, beyond thinking requires diligent practice.

Circle of Sound stretching, rooting, and movement exercises are a way of practicing "doerless doing." Martha Graham said about the art of dance: "All that is important is this one moment in movement . . . Do not let it slip away unnoticed and unused." Be with the body as you stretch, as you root and as you move through the *taijiquan* form. Your stretching, rooting, and movement practice can give rise to your capacity to "let go" of the tension in your body and mind. You may realize that things are already perfectly what they should be.

Preparing the Body to Sing

We usually prepare the body with stretching exercises before proceeding with the *Circle of Sound* core practice. Lots of stretching some days, less on others. These simple stretching exercises are offered here to give you additional resources in varying your warm-up routine.

It is not absolutely necessary to use all of the stretches presented here. Please add stretches you are comfortable with, providing that they contribute to a deeper "body knowing" and do not inhibit the singers' ability to find their center.

Some very common warm-ups I see in choirs can actually get in the way of preparing for singing. For instance, I find the practice of having a line of singers turn sideways and each massage the shoulders of the person in front of them can add tension to rather than relax the body. To massage the person in front of me, I need to tighten the muscles in my shoulders, arms, and hands, and if I have to lean to reach that person, my lower back and legs also tighten. On top of this, the person behind massaging me is busily transferring his own muscle tension and hectic day into my shoulders.

Closing the Circle

As you grow in your understanding of these movement practices, pay attention to what each exercise does in terms of body connection, breath awareness, and relaxation. Are you ready to sing? As we said earlier, singers are their own best teachers.

The purpose of these stretching exercises is to bring about awareness of the body and prepare for singing. Following are some points to help you with the stretches.

The teacher-conductor should:

1. **Invite the singers to mindfully stand and spread out**, a little more than an arm's length distance away from the next singer in the available space.

2. **Remind the singers to breathe and be mindful** as they stretch. The quality of the breath determines the quality and speed of the movement. If the singers seem to be rushing through these stretches, it is likely that they are holding their breath while they move and are in a hurry to get to the end so they can breathe!

3. **Encourage singers to treat stretching as a welcome opportunity** to pay attention to how their feet are touching the floor, how soft their shoulders are, how relaxed their jaw is, how relaxed their hands are, etc., rather than "do this because I say so" direction.

4. **Work together in time** so that all participants are close to the same place within a given stretch. This helps build connections among members of the chorus, but please do not rigidly impose these connections. Let it develop organically.

5. **Remember to move *slowly***, and whichever of these exercises you do, repeat them at least three times.

6. **You can also use contextual phrases from your current repertoire**. This can help connect body movement to the musical experience. For example, say "**harmony** and **grace**" (Bernstein: "There Is a Garden") as you swing your arms from side to side. Don't force such connections, and if there are none in your repertoire at the moment, that is just fine!

7. **Even if you skip some of these stretches, still try to do the ones you have chosen in the order they are presented here**. For example, use stretches 1, 4, 6, and 7 rather than stretches 6, 4, 1, and 7.

> *A word of caution:* Please be thoughtful and careful about all stretching. Do not overdo it. At the beginning of a session, always offer the opportunity for people to not do a stretch or exercise that they are not comfortable with. Always move slowly, stay relaxed, and remember to breathe!

Closing the Circle

Stretching Exercises

1. Swinging arms side to side (keep arms & hands soft)

2. Rolling head down and to each side (not all the way around)

Closing the Circle

Stretching Exercises

3. Head side to side
(as in shaking your head "no")

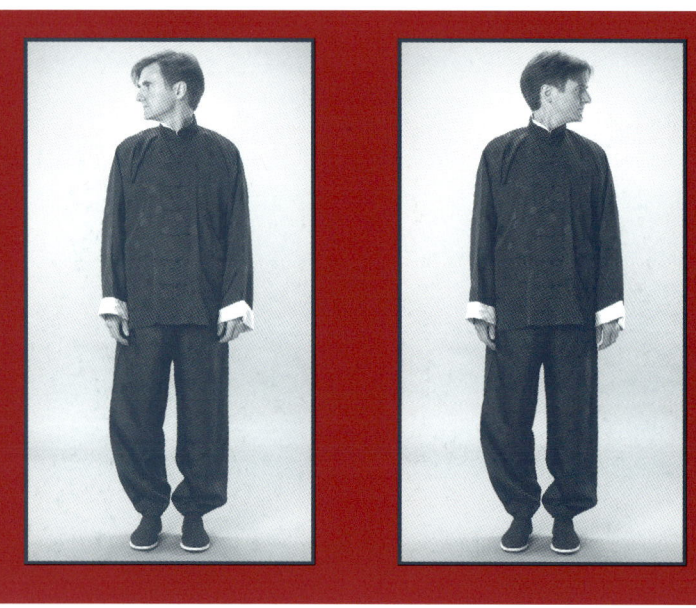

4. Head up and down
(as in nodding "yes")

5. Circling shoulders up and backwards
(keep arms and hands soft)

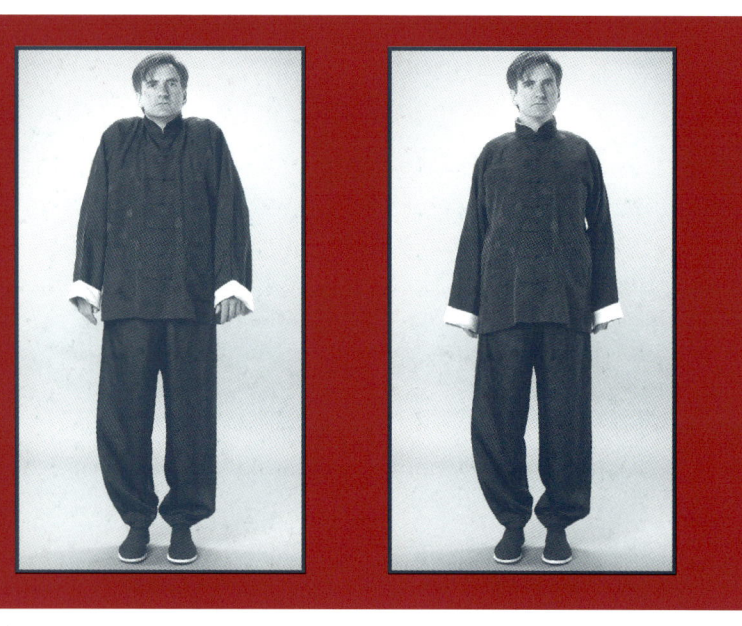

6. Circling shoulders up and forwards
(keep arms and hands soft)

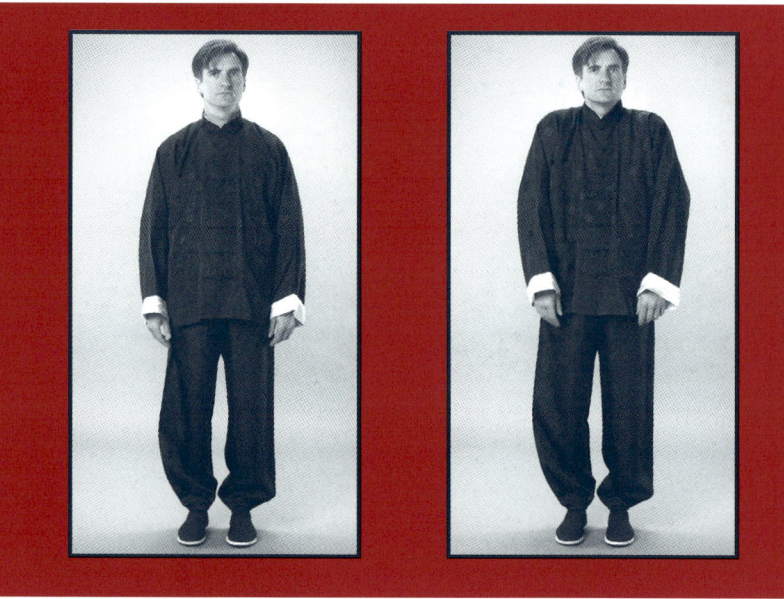

Closing the Circle

Stretching Exercises

7. Circling shoulders in opposite directions (one goes up as the other goes down)—do both directions

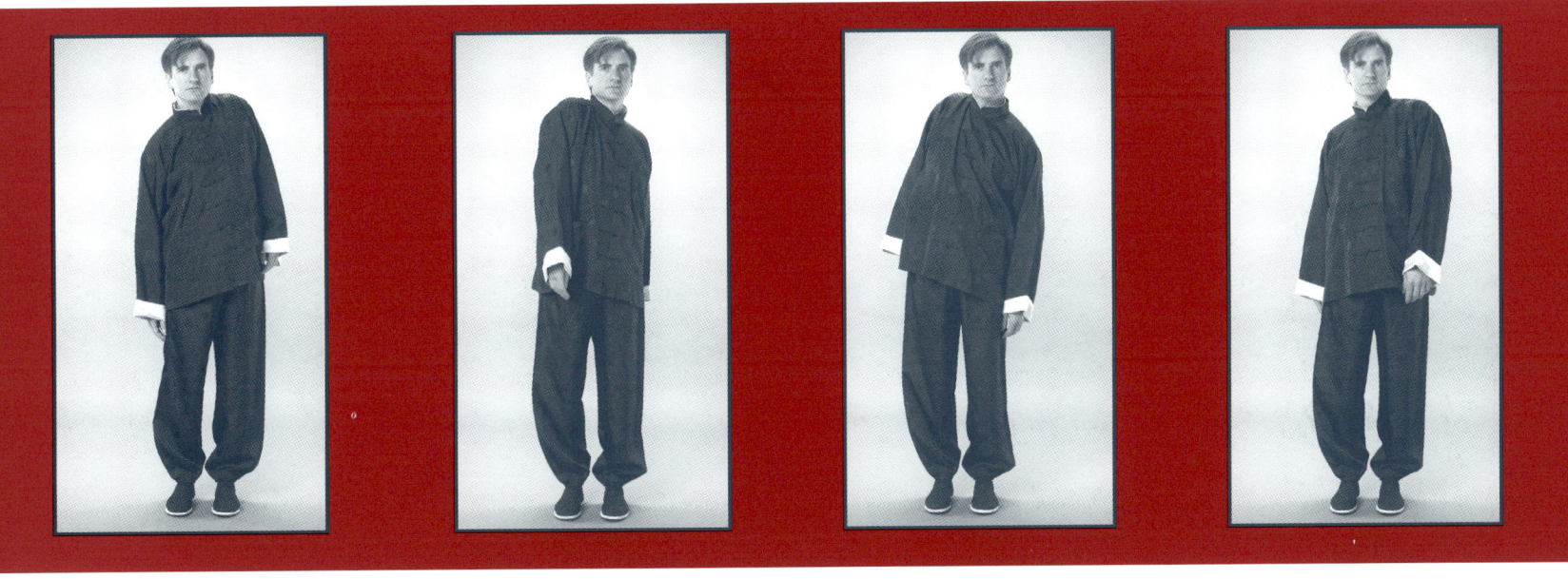

8. Arms opening and closing (allow chest and shoulder blades to move)

Closing the Circle

Stretching Exercises

9. Bending sideways (palms up) (keep arms & hands soft)

10. Circling hips—feet together (head and feet stay in place as the hips circle)

Closing the Circle

Stretching Exercises

11. Circling hips—feet apart (head and feet stay in place as the hips circle)(keep arms & hands soft)

12A. Touching toes—feet together—(center)
(come back to the center each time and as you rise up, keep your hands close to your body)

Closing the Circle

Stretching Exercises

12B. Touching toes—feet together—(right)

12C. Touching toes—feet together—(left)

Closing the Circle

Stretching Exercises

13. Circling knees (rotate the leg with a little weight on the ball of the foot)

14. Stretching back of legs—toe up and toe down (weight mostly on back leg)

Closing the Circle

Taijiquan Form

The practice of *taijiquan* form (t'ai chi ch'uan) is about the flow of energy through a sequence of smooth, continuous circular movements. The movement form we have adapted for *Circle of Sound* is both horizontal and vertical, it flows in and out on the breath. Together, these continuous circular movements create energy for maintaining the balance between yin (ease, softness) and yang (firm, strong). *Taijiquan* practice contributes to the singer's ability to balance his actions. The gross body movements of this form send messages from the energy sources outside and around the body to the energy sources inside the body. As the body roots and slowly moves from one posture to another without any breaks, hesitations or sudden changes, the vocal tract or resonance chamber within the body develops a similar sensibility. The continuity of letting one slow movement flow smoothly into the next slow movement will send a "circle" message to the voice. The practice of these slow smooth movements centers the body, softens the body, calms the spirit and prepares the whole person for singing as "non-doing" (*wu-wei*).

This is the beginning portion of the *taijiquan* form that I practice. This material is meant only as a taste of what *taijiquan* can be, and not as a definitive guide to the whole art form.

We have found that teaching *taijiquan* principles in the context of a traditional form is the best way to deepen vocal students' understanding of the intentional movements presented in *Circle of Sound Voice Education*. The Intentional Movements presented in Chapter 3 are not *taijiquan* per se—they are not movements taken directly from a *taijiquan* form but, rather, they are informed by the underlying principles of *taijiquan* such as circularity and movement connected to breath.

Concept of Wuji

When we finish the stretching exercises and before breathing meditation or the *taijiquan* form begins, we encourage students to relax their bodies into a *wuji* posture. The *wuji* posture feels like the body is standing in a sitting position. The center of gravity is a little lower than what might be considered normal Western style standing up straight.

Once the students find and feel the benefits of *wuji* posture, they can stand or sit for the breathing meditation. If the students are sitting, they should sit at the front of their chairs with their feet planted firmly on the ground and their hands softly in their laps. When the student sits for breathing meditation and singing, the posture feels like they are standing. In typically Zen style, and the harmonious interplay of opposite forces, the singer stands in a sitting posture and sits in a standing posture.

Wuji Posture for Singing

Before doing the *taijiquan* form, we begin with *quiet standing*, which is also referred to as *wuji* or *void stance*. The purpose of quiet standing is to settle the breath, calm the mind, and center the body. It is a great practice for lowering your center of gravity and "rooting" into the earth. It helps develop a center from which all actions can emanate with power and consistency.

As well as serving as a preparation for doing a *taijiquan* form, *quiet standing* can be practiced on its own. Many *taijiquan* teachers say this simple daily practice of *wuji* for five to fifteen minutes can bring great vitality and energy.

Breath Center or Dantien

Closing the Circle

For both adult and youth choirs, we use three to five minutes of quiet standing at the beginning of a rehearsal. The time spent brings great dividends throughout the rehearsal. Increased concentration and a quiet focus allow the student's mind and body to work together with purpose and confidence.

Wuji Preparation

Wuji posture involves three steps. The first two are preparation—finding your breath center and positioning your stance—and the third is the standing itself.

Your breath center or *dantien* is approximately three finger-widths below your navel and halfway between the front and back of your body. Place your hands on this point and allow your breath to sink until it feels like it is rising and falling under your hands. Please do not force the breath into your breath center. Allow it to go there naturally. Next time you are around a baby, take a moment to feel where he is breathing. Of course, make sure you know the baby—don't try this on a stranger's baby!

Wuji posture

Positioning Your Stance

These *wuji* posture directions will help you adjust your body for optimum posture.

Feet (Rooted)

- Shoulder-width apart, or a little narrower
- Toes pointed forward, parallel
- Flat on the ground with weight evenly distributed

Experiment with how it feels to have your weight mostly on your heels (back), on your toes (forward), on the outside, on the inside. Use the feedback from this experiment to learn the feeling of having your weight evenly distributed.

Knees (Softened)

- Bent gently and in line with your feet (which are pointed forward)

Aim for a softness in your stance; do not force yourself to sink too low or hold yourself up. Aim for a soft gentle bend. This should not feel difficult if you are not forcing it.

Hips (Relaxed)

- In line with the center of your feet
- Coccyx tucked under so your lower back is flat

The coccyx is the base of the tailbone. "Flat" back means that if you were lying on the floor, there would be little or no space between your lower back and the floor.

Shoulders (Soft)

- Relaxed
- In line with the center of your feet
- Chest relaxed

Circle of Sound Voice Education • 91

Closing the Circle

Arms and Hands (Easy)
- Arms at your side with a little space (about the size of an egg) between your arms and your body
- Hands soft and relaxed with palms facing slightly backwards

Head (Loose)
- Imagine that the top of your head is being suspended from a string, or that it is rising up like a balloon
- Eyes looking straight ahead, slightly below horizontal, with a soft focus
- Jaw relaxed
- Tip of your tongue lightly touching the roof of your mouth, just behind the teeth

(The observation of placing the tongue just behind the teeth is for standing posture but works well for breathing meditation, too.)

Standing

Once you are in a comfortable, rooted position come back to your breath center and observe the breath as it rises and falls. Remember to *allow* the breath to rise and fall on its own. Check your breath by placing one hand on the abdomen (breath center) or *dantien*) and feeling the rise and fall of the abdomen as you *breathe-in* and *breath-out*. (See "Breath Center" photo on page 86.)

Introduction to Taijiquan: A Beginning Form

The following descriptions give some detail of the *taijiquan* movement form and some points to watch for as you do the sequenced movements. Demonstrations of exercises follow descriptions and begin on page 94

> **Knee Alignment:** *During all of these movements, it is very important to keep the knees aligned with the toes. Do not allow the knees to fall sideways.*

Begin with Quiet Stance (Wuji)
- Stand for a few minutes to center yourself.

1. Opening
- Arms rising from sides to shoulder level, attention on back of hands. Once they reach the top, they begin downward without a break in the movement (no pause at the top), attention on the palms.
- Keep the shoulders down and relaxed.
- Hands soft and relaxed.
- Do this movement any number of times (e.g., three to nine)

2. Rolling The Ball
- Left palm facing down over right palm facing up—like you are holding a basketball (or a smaller ball)—in front of the abdomen and slightly away from the body.
- Turn waist to left no more than 45°, keeping the hands in front of the abdomen.
- Roll ball over so the right hand is on top, and then turn waist 45° to the right.
- Roll ball over so the left hand is on top, and then turn waist 45° to the left.
- Continue this sequence at least three times and then move to the next step.

Closing the Circle

- Keep elbows out from the body. There will be a tendency to let the following elbow collapse into the body.
- Allow hands to stay soft and relaxed. Hold onto the "ball" gently.

3. Ward Off Left

- On the last time you roll the ball to the left, shift the weight onto the left foot.
- Roll the ball over so the right hand is on top. Turn waist to the right, allowing the right foot to pivot on the heel 45° to the right.
- Shift all weight onto the right foot while holding the ball in front of the right hip.
- When the left leg is empty, lift it and step straight ahead a comfortable distance—not too far, and not too little.
- Shift forward until left shin is perpendicular and at the same time allow the left arm to raise (palm facing you) until it is across the body at about the level of the sternum. Right hand lowers slightly with palm facing the earth Shoulders square to the front.

4. Ward Off Right

- From left ward off, shift the weight back onto the right, letting the left toe lift but keeping the heel on the ground.
- Turn the waist and the left foot 45° to the right. Shift the weight onto the left foot while holding the ball in front of the left hip—left hand over right hand.
- Step straight ahead with the right foot (this is 90° right from the direction you began in). Shift forward until right shin is perpendicular to the floor.
- Allow the right arm to rise to sternum level, palm facing you.
- Left hand palm-down, slightly lower than right forearm.

5. Pull Back

- While turning the waist 45° to the right, rotate right palm up and continue to let left palm face the earth.
- When 45° is reached, begin to turn waist 90° to the left and sit back on the left leg.
- Arms should follow waist in a counter-clockwise circle.

6. Press

- When weight is on left leg and ready to come forward again, allow the arms to collapse slightly toward the body as they begin to move forward, continuing along the path. Attach left palm to right wrist and shift the weight forward until the right leg is perpendicular to the floor. Press outward slightly with the hands.

7. Push

- Shift the weight back and open the arms to shoulder width, palms facing each other, keeping elbows down.
- Shift the weight forward until the right leg is perpendicular to the floor, palms facing forward.

8. Single Whip

- Shift the weight backwards, raising right toe but keeping the heel on the ground. Rotate left palm to face you. Right hand into beak hand—all fingertips and thumbs together. Keep wrist straight.
- Rotate waist and right foot 45° to the left.
- Shift the weight in the direction of the right foot until left foot is empty.
- Anchoring right hand and right leg, step with left leg and place heel on the same plane as right foot. Continue to turn waist to left allowing left hand to cross at face level and rotating counterclockwise until it is palm out and the weight is 60 percent on the left.
- Arms should be in line with the hips and the elbows should be pointing downward.

9. Closing

- Shift to either right or left foot, bring arms and feet together, and lower arms to side. This sets the *taijiquan* movement down rather than dropping it or throwing it away.

Remember this is a very short portion of this particular *taijiquan* form. The complete form takes anywhere from 30—40 minutes, depending on the pace.

Closing the Circle

Begin with Quiet Stance (Wuji)

1. Opening

2. Rolling the Ball

3. Ward Off Left

Closing the Circle

4. Ward Off Right

5. Pull Back

6. Press

Circle of Sound Voice Education • 95

# Closing the Circle

7. Push

8. Single Whip

9. Closing

Closing the Circle

Studying Taijiquan

If you wish to explore *taijiquan* further, there are many good books available and many good teachers throughout the world. It is best to learn directly from a teacher. Take the same care in choosing a *taijiquan* teacher as you would choosing a private music teacher for yourself or your child. Look for a good practitioner, of course, but also for good pedagogy and a kind spirit. You should be able to progress at a pace that is best for you and not have to learn a specific number of movements per class. (Quality, not quantity.) It took me more than a year to learn the sequence of moves that make up the form I practice (and I am still working on understanding them), but I have had students learn the sequence in only five to six months.

While there is no accreditation body for teachers of *taijiquan*, you can ask questions. A prospective teacher should have been studying and practicing for at least four to six years and have some knowledge of Taoist philosophy (theory) and the *taiji* classics. The *taiji* classics are a number of must-read texts that give insight into the meaning of the movements, forms, and the art. The teacher should have an understanding of push hands (which could be described as a gentle type of sparring) and also understand the martial applications of the movements, yet not feel a need to always demonstrate them on you. Beginning students should learn form and principles and, as they progress, learn some simple push hands circling. A beginning student should not engage in more complex push hands or sparring, as this could undermine the training that is occurring in the form. A beginning student will rely on old ways and habits of moving to deal with an "opponent" because the *taijiquan* training is not yet deep enough to rely upon.

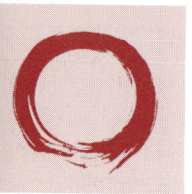

Closing the Circle

Cultivating Happiness
—Doreen Rao

In closing the Circle, I confess that since I began practicing conscious breathing and *taijiquan* on a regular basis, I am a better teacher and a happier person. It's not that I wasn't a good teacher before, or that I suffered from being unhappy. It's simply that as my body began to enjoy the slow and continuous movements of t'ai chi, and my mind savored the calm and concentration of breathing meditation, I grew personally in my ability to listen deeply and to be fully present to others. Artistically, the benefits of this contemplative practice included my ability to diagnose musical and emotional problems in lessons and rehearsals. My concentration improved and I found memorization easy. As skeptic journalist Joel Stein wrote in the cover article of a recent issue of *Time*, "Scientists study it. Doctors recommend it. Millions of Americans . . . practice it every day. Why? Because meditation works."

Combined, adapted, and sequenced as a simple and accessible approach to voice education, *taijiquan* and mindfulness meditation constitute the contemplative foundation for *Circle of Sound Voice Education*. If indeed singing constitutes a way of being in the world, and if being healthy is fundamental to being happy, this easy and attainable approach to singing belongs to everyone.

Voice education is not just about singing beautiful tones or making perfect performances. It is about voicing our concern for people, it is about community-making, and it represents a dynamic complex of personal understanding, human tolerance, and social justice. It is about developing inner peace and well-being. It is about relationship-making. It is about honoring diversity and serving others. With *Circle of Sound Voice Education*, the practice of singing is the practice of awareness, mindfulness, deep listening, and well-being. Singing is about the art of cultivating happiness.

In closing, we return to the words of Jalal Al-Din Rumi:

> *Don't worry about saving these songs!*
> *And if one of our instruments breaks,*
> *it doesn't matter.*
>
> *We have fallen into the place*
> *where everything is music.*
>
> —Rumi
> *from "Where Everything is Music"*

About the Authors

Doreen Rao, Ph.D.
Conductor–Master Teacher

Doreen Rao's distinguished career as conductor and master teacher links the standards of professional performance with the goals of music education. Celebrated for her spirited and moving concerts and her conducting master classes, Rao's commitment to choral music education is recognized in her worldwide appearances and in her award-winning publications with Boosey & Hawkes.

As the University of Toronto Elmer Iseler Chair in Conducting, Rao directs the University's MacMillan Singers and Chamber Singers. Her award-winning choirs enjoy regular performance collaborations with the Toronto Symphony Orchestra, the University Symphony Orchestra, and the University of Toronto's professional choir-in-residence, the Elmer Iseler Singers.

During her long association with the Chicago Symphony Orchestra, Rao served as assistant conductor of the Chicago Symphony Chorus under Margaret Hillis, her teacher and mentor. As music director of the celebrated Glen Ellyn Children's Chorus, Rao prepared her choirs for concerts and recorded performances that won four Grammy Awards and a Grand Prix du Disque under Sir Georg Solti, Claudio Abbado, Margaret Hillis, and James Levine.

Recognized as one of the world's leading experts on children's and youth choirs, Rao founded the American Choral Directors Association's National Committee on Children's Choirs, which

inspired the children's choir movement in America. In a national tribute presented to her by the American Choral Directors Association, the eminent Robert Shaw wrote: "The world of choral music owes her special thanks. She is preparing our future." Canadian journalist Bronwyn Drainie described Rao as a brilliant artist and teacher "whose methods and materials could re-energize the art of choral singing."

Rao was educated in the United States, earning her master's degree in voice and Ph.D. in aesthetics from Northwestern University. She is the recipient of numerous honors and awards including those from the Phi Mu Alpha Sinfonia for "her significant and lasting contributions to the cause of American music," the American Choral Directors Association

About the Authors

for "her commitment to choral excellence," and the YWCA for "her outstanding leadership in Arts and Culture."

Rao is the founder and artistic director of the New Millennium Festival Concerts and the CME Institute for Choral Teacher Education, dynamic and innovative performance and professional development programs for choirs, conductors, teachers, and composers. She enjoys a full life of family, friends, students, and colleagues in Toronto and around the world. See: www.choralmusicexperience.com or www.doreenrao.com.

Bill Perison
T'ai-Chi Teacher, Composer and Music Technology Consultant

Bill Perison has practiced and taught *taijiquan* for 17 years. After earning a bachelor of fine arts degree in music from York University in Toronto, Canada, he studied *taijiquan* with Andy James at Emerge Internal Arts Center, one of Toronto's foremost martial arts schools. At United States martial arts competitions he has won gold and bronze medals for both his presentation of his form and his skills in push-hands matches.

Perison integrates his music and martial arts background by sharing with performing artists the body/mind/spirit freedom gained through *taijiquan*. This training helps musicians develop and expand their creative potential. He teaches relaxation and body/mind connection to conductors and singers at Doreen Rao's Choral Music Experience Institute for Choral Teacher Education and at workshops throughout North America and Europe.

As a composer and performer Perison has recorded *Coconut Tree*, an album of original music and stories for children. He has performed in Canada and the United States and has been featured on CBC radio. His choral works have been published by Boosey and Hawkes, including an arrangement of his song "Magic Land" from *Coconut Tree*.

Perison lives on Vancouver Island in British Columbia, Canada, with his wife and twin sons. He can be contacted at www.billperison.ca.

Notes

Foreword

1. Roland Barthes, *The Grain of the Voice* (New York: Hill & Wang, 1985), p. 243.

2. C. Keil and S. Feld, *Music Grooves* (Chicago: University of Chicago Press, 1994).

3. Ludwig Wittgenstein, *Philosophical Investigations* (New York: Macmillan, 1958).

Preface

1. Coleman Barks, *The Essential Rumi* (San Francisco: Harper, 1995), p. 34.

2. Thich Nhat Hanh, *Peace Is Every Step: The Path of Mindfulness in Everyday Life* (New York: Bantam Books, 1992), pp. 8–10.

Chapter 1

1. *Choral Music Experience* is a vocal performance approach to music teaching and learning. Developed by Doreen Rao as an instructional resource for choral program planning, curriculum design and concert performance, the CME choral music series was first published in 1986 by Boosey & Hawkes. The CME performance model and the culturally diverse instructional repertoire were developed in response to the prevailing criticism that choral singing in music education had little "real" educational value. The *Choral Music Experience* performance approach to music teaching and learning is based on a philosophy of singing as a way of "being" musical. It suggests that singing distinctive and culturally diverse repertoire taught in a reflective and empowering manner is a means of developing self awareness, mindfulness, deep listening and well-being.

2. From an inscription on a 19th-century rattle fragment found in the Northwest Coast of Canada as referenced by Joan Halifax in *Shaman: The Wounded Healer* (London: Thames and Hudson, Ltd., 1982, out of print) p. 58.

3. Conversation between Margaret Tilly and C.G. Jung reported by Patricia Warming in "The Use of Music in Jungian Analysis," *Open Ear Journal* (2000): p. 149.

4. Attributed to C.G. Jung from *The Symbolic Life* in a book by Christine Baldwin, *Calling the Circle: The First and Future Culture* (New York, Bantam Books: 1994), p. 29.

5. Francis Sparshott, "Conceptual Aspects of Music Education," in *The New Grove Dictionary of Music and Musicians*, ed. Stanley Sadie (London: Macmillan, 1980), p. 56.

6. Ibid.

7. Martin Buber, *I and Thou* (New York: Charles Scribner and Sons, 1970), pp. 31–33.

Notes

8. Thich Nhat Hanh, *Interbeing: Fourteen Guidelines for Engaged Buddhism*, 3rd ed. (Berkeley, California: Parallax Press, 1998).

Chapter 3

1. Hanh, *Peace Is Every Step*, p. 9.

2. Thomas Moore, *The Re-Enchantment of Everyday Life* (New York: HarperCollins, 1996), p. 220.

3. A meditation with Joan Halifax Roshi on Cortez Island, British Columbia, May 1997.

4. Doreen Rao in conversation with conducting student Debra Piotrowski at the University of Toronto CME Institute for Choral Teacher Education, July 2000.

Chapter 4

1. Daniel Goleman, *Emotional Intelligence* (New York: Bantam Books, 1995), p. xiii.

2. David Best's view is reported by Wayne Bowman in his article "Educating Musically" in *The New Handbook of Research on Music Teaching and Learning; Project of the Music Educators National Conference*, eds. Richard Cowell and Carol Richardson (New York: Oxford University Press, 2002).

3. An excellent but unfortunately out-of-print book is Small's *Musicking: The Meanings of Performing and Listening* (Lebanon, NH: University Press of New England: 1998).

4. Aristotle, The Nicomachean Ethics (New York: Oxford University Press, 1998).

Chapter 5

1. Joel Stein, "The Science of Meditation," *Time*, 4 August 2003: p. 52.

2. This idea was inspired by Wayne Bowman's pioneering work in the area of music education philosophy. His article "Educating Musically" in *The New Handbook of Research on Music Teaching and Learning* (see Chap. 4, note 2 above) discusses the concept of phronesis, which he describes as *an ethical disposition upon which musical practice rests*. If I understand Wayne's explanation of phronesis as a consideration for music education, singing as a human practice is part of one's character, inseparable from one's identity. The singer's character and identity is embodied in her voice. "This ethical mode of being present to otherness does not take its guidance from some detached intellectual regulatory mechanism but from one's entire being." (p. 24 of the pre-publication manuscript).

3. From the introduction to John Robert Colombo's *Poems of the Inuit* (Ottawa: Oberon Press, 1981, out of print, p. 13), as remembered by Knud Rasmussen, who lived in the Arctic with Orpingalik in the 1920s.

4. Quoted by Doreen Rao in *Craft, Singing Craft and Musical Experience* (Ann Arbor, MI: U.M.I. Dissertation Information Service, 1988), p. 142.

5. Ibid.

6. Thomas Merton, *The Other Side of the Mountain: The End of the Journey* (San Francisco: Harper, 1998).

7. Manfred Clynes, "On Healing and Music" in *Music Physician for Times to Come*, ed. Don Campbell (Wheaton, IL: Quest Books, 1992), p. 121.

8. Ibid.

9. I recommend Jon Kabit-Zinn's *Wherever You Go—There You Are: Mindfulness Meditation in Everyday Life* (New York: Hyperion, 1995) to my students and colleagues interested in mindfulness practice.

10. This work and the extensive research being done today is discussed by Marshall Glickman in "The Lama and the Lab," *Tricycle* 12, no. 3 (2003): pp. 70–74.

Notes

11. Heather Eyerly is currently completing her doctoral research at the University of Toronto Faculty of Music. She currently serves as assistant professor of music education at The Crane School of Music, SUNY–Potsdam.

12. Reported by Beverly J. Ogdon, "Bel Canto Training in Niccolo Porpora's England with a Twentieth-Century Rationale" in *The Phenomenon of Singing 2* (Newfoundland, Canada: Memorial University, 1999), p. 174.

13. Stuart M. Silverman, M.D., "New Frontiers in Classical Music Performance," *Open Ear Journal* (2000): pp. 113–117.

14. I met Professor Mihalyi Csikszentmihalyi in Chicago during the early stages of my doctoral research at Northwestern University. His research at the University of Chicago came to my attention in "Phylogenetic and Ontogenetic Functions of Artistic Cognition" in *The Arts, Cognition and Basic Skills*, edited by Stanley S. Madeja (St. Louis: CMEREL, 1978). He has written *Beyond Boredom and Anxiety* (San Francisco: Jossey-Bass, 1975) and with his wife Isabella Csikszentmihalyi (eds.) he gave us *Optimal Experience: Psychological Studies of Flow in Consciousness* (Cambridge: Cambridge University Press, 1988). His national best seller is *Flow: The Psychology of Optimal Experience* (New York: HarperCollins, 1991). This theory was reported and discussed by me in *Craft, Singing Craft and Musical Experience*, 1988.

15. The comparison of Csikszentmihalyi's flow theory with Zen Buddhism was made by Andrew Cooper in "The Man Who Found the Flow," *Shambala Sun*, September 1998: pp. 24–61.

16. Wayne Bowman, *Philosophical Perspectives on Music* (New York: Oxford University Press, 1998).

17. Bowman, "Educating Musically."

18. Ibid.

19. Ibid.

20. John P. Miller, *Holistic Teacher* (Toronto: The Ontario Institute for Standards in Education Press, Curriculum Series/65, 1993).

21. The benefits of singing are discussed by Susan Elizabeth Hale in her interesting book *Song and Silence: Voicing the Soul* (Albuquerque, NM: La Alameda Press, 1995).

Bibliography

Recommended Reading

Publications by Doreen Rao

Rao, Doreen. *We Will Sing! Choral Music Experience for Classroom Choirs*. New York: Boosey & Hawkes, 1994.

———. *Artistry in Music Education*. CME Library, Volume 1. New York: Boosey & Hawkes, 1987.

———. *The Artist in Every Child*. CME Library, Volume 2. New York: Boosey & Hawkes, 1988.

———. *The Art in Choral Music*. CME Library, Volume 3. New York: Boosey & Hawkes, 1990.

———. *Teaching Children Through Choral Music Experience*. CME Library, Volume 4. New York: Boosey & Hawkes, 1991.

———. *The Young Singing Voice*. 2nd ed. CME Library, Volume 5. New York: Boosey & Hawkes, 1987.

———. *Choral Music for Children: An Annotated List*. Reston. Virginia: Music Educators National Conference (MENC), 1990. (A single file copy library is available through AMC Music, Attn: Martha Palmer, 3330 Hilcroft, Suite H, Houston, TX 77057)

———, co-author. *SING!* A choral music textbook for secondary school music. Houston: Hinshaw Music Textbook Division, 1987.

———, editor. *Choral Journal* Special Issue on the Children's Choir. March, 1989, Vol. 29, No. 8. (Available through the American Choral Director's Association National Headquarters, P.O. Box 6310, Lawton, OK, 73506-0130, USA).

———. "Choral Singing and American Music Education Today." *International Choral Bulletin*, April, 1993.

———. "Selected Repertoire for Children's Chorus and Orchestra." *Research Memorandum Series*, 142, The American Choral Foundation, August, 1986.

———. "Children's Treble Voices: Interview with Sir David Willcocks." *Choral Journal*, March, 1985.

———. "Extended Choral Works for Treble Voices." *Choral Journal*, December, 1982.

Rao, Doreen and David Elliot. "Musical Performance and Music Education." *Design for Arts in Education*, May/June 1990, Vol. 91, No. 5.

Mindfulness

Hanh, Thich Nhat. *Interbeing: Fourteen Guidelines for Engaged Buddhism*. Berkeley, California: Parallax Press, 1998 (3rd ed.).

Hanh, Thich Nhat. *Peace Is Every Step: The Path of Mindfulness in Everyday Life*. New York: Bantam Books, 1992.

Kabit-Zinn, Jon. *Wherever You Go—There You Are: Mindfulness Meditation in Everyday Life*. New York: Hyperion, 1995.

Taijiquan

Although there are many books out about *taijiquan* these two are a good place to begin:

Ch'ing, Chen Man. *Cheng Tzu's Thirteen Treatises on T'ai Chi Ch'uan*. Berkeley, CA: North Atlantic Books, 1985.

Jou, Tsung Hwa. *The Dao of Taijiquan: Way to Rejuvenation*. Boston, MA: Tuttle Publishing, 1998 (3rd ed.).

Teacher-Conductor Resources

Bartle, Jean Ashworth. *Lifeline for Children's Choir Directors*. Toronto: Gordon V. Thompson, 1988.

Elliott, Daivd J. *Music Matters: A New Philosophy of Music Education*. New York: Oxford University Press, 1995.

Elliott, David, J. "When I Sing: The Nature and Value of Choral Music Education." *Choral Journal,* March, 1993, Vol. 33, No. 8.

Fowler, Charles, ed. *The Crane Symposium: Toward an Understanding of the Teaching and Learning of Music Performance*. Potsdam. NY: Potsdam College of the State University of New York.

Kemp, Helen. *Vocal Methods for the Children's Choir*. Philadelphia: Fortress Press, 1965.

Phillips, Kenneth. *Teaching Kids to Sing*. New York: MacMillan, 1992.

Pohjola, Erkki. *The Tapiola Sound*. Ft Lauderdale, FL: Walton Music Corp, 1993.

Szönyi, Erzsébet. *Kodály's Principles in Practice*. New York: Boosey & Hawkes, 1979.

Tacka, Philip, and Micheál Houlahan. *Sound Thinking. Music Skill Development Through The Kodály Concept.*. 2 vols. New York: Boosey & Hawkes, 1993.

Tacka, Philip, and Micheál Houlahan. *Sound Thinking. Music for Sight-Singing and Ear Training*. 2 vols. New York: Boosey & Hawkes, 1990.

Tagg, Barbara and Linda Ferriera (guest editors). *Choral Journal* Special Issue on the Children's Choir. March, 1993, Vol. 33, No. 8. (Available through the American Choral Director's Association National Headquarters, P.O. Box 6310, Lawton, OK, 73506-0130, USA).